Instant Vortex Air Fryer Oven Cookbook

Easy and Healthy Recipes to Air Fryer, Roasting, Broiling, Baking,

Reheating, Dehydrating, and Rotisserie.

Randon Banker

Table of contents

Chapter 1: Understanding the Instant Plus Vortex Air Fryer Oven

Instant Kitchen Appliances have come up with yet another amazing surprise for all the homemakers and made cooking easier than ever before. Though Instant Pot has already introduced ranges of kitchen appliances, which have revolutionized the concept of smart cooking, now Instant Pot has gone one step ahead and brought a Vortex Air Fryer oven for its customers. How this vortex Air fryer oven is different from all other ovens in the market? Well, that will be shortly discussed in this cookbook, along with all the recipes that you can cook well in this new vortex oven. One thing that can be said with the looks of this Air fryer oven is that now you can manage to cook, roast, bake, air fryer and do much in the capacious one-unit appliance. Whether it is roasting a whole chicken or Air frying the pork chops, everything can be cooked in no time with the new vortex heat technology in the Instant Plus Vortex Air fryer oven.

The Benefits of Using Instant Plus Vortex Air Fryer Oven

Since there are several Air fryer ovens available in the market, let us tell you how the Instant Plus vortex Air fryer oven stands out from the rest.

1. Turn and Flip Indicator

The special feature that has been added to the Instant Plus vortex is the Turn and flip indicator. Now the user need not to constantly check the food inside and keep track of time as to when to rotate or flip the food, with this smart feature the Air fryer oven will itself lit the TURN sign on the screen to indicate that its time to flip the food or toss it.

2. 6 in One Air Fryer Oven

The Air fryer oven is designed with six smart cooking features:

- Air Fry
- Roast
- Broil
- Bake
- Reheat
- Dehydrate

Each of these modes has its default cooking time and temperatures which can be adjusted using function keys. With its one-touch technology, the unit can be switched to one mode to another easily.

3. Rotisserie Cooking

The feature that is making the most buzz among the Instant users is the special basket that can be fixed to cook rotisserie chicken. It keeps the rotating chicken on the rotisserie rod while it is cooked evenly from all the sides. The vortex heating mechanism provides heat from the top and cooks the meat down to every grain while giving a crispy layer on the outside. With Air fryer oven now, you don't need to set up a BBQ grill to roast a whole chicken, you can do that right in your kitchen.

4. Energy and Time Efficient

The Instant Vortex plus cook's food by creating a hot vortex of air inside the oven. This means that no overcooking, burning, or undercooking of food. The heating element is fixed in the upper portion of the oven, uses 1500 MW of power. The direct and even heat saves both time and energy; and cooks food quickly.

5. Capacious

Unlike other electric ovens, you will find Instant Vortex Plus Air fryer oven much capacious and suitable to cook large serving sizes, whether it is a whole chicken or duck, so you can easily put them on the rotisserie rod. The interior of the oven is large enough to carry a rotisserie basket and large-sized baking pans. The sizes vary for each model; you can get from 7 to 10 quartz of the Instant Air fryer oven as per your need.

6. User-Friendly

There are no rotating dials or complex mechanisms to control the functional and operational keys of this oven. The control panel has the program's keys and the keys to adjust the time and temperature. The user can change the settings by a single press of the button and can also go for the default setting of each program.

Structural Composition of the Instant Plus Vortex Air Fryer Oven

An Instant Plus Vortex Air fryer oven comes with several accessories to ease out the cooking process. Inside its box, you will find plenty of useful utensils. Whenever you buy the product, make sure to check the component and see if it is instant and working properly. An Instant Plus Vortex Air Fryer Oven box comes with:

- Instant Vortex Air Fryer Oven
- Drip pan
- 2 cooking trays
- rotisserie spit and forks
- rotisserie basket
- rotisserie fetch tool

Set the oven on a flat and even surface after unboxing. Make sure to keep it away from other appliances and do not cover its top vent with anything. The oven is designed to place on the countertops, avoid placing it in any outdoor setting. Once the base unit is set, remove all its accessories like the baskets, cooking trays and pan etc. and wash them well before the first use. The accessories should be dried well before cooking.

Unit Specifications:

The Instant Vortex Plus Air Fryer oven we are unboxing here has the following features. The other Vortex models vary in size and the capacity of their interior but they all have similar cooking features and smart operations.

Size: 10 Quart

Heating Element: 1500W Heating Element

Dimensions in: 13.23L x 13.23W x 14.37H

Weight: 16.94 lbs.

Power supply: 120V – 60Hz

Maximum Draw: 1500 Watts

Power Supply Cord :1.2 meters, hardwired, grounded polarized plug

Every Instant Pot Vortex Air fryer oven comes with a 12 months working-warrantee, which is enough to understand the device and check it up to its best use. The exterior of the unit is made out of stainless steel and its interior is well insulated enclosed by a removable door on the front.

The Control Panel:

The control panel of the Instant vortex Air fryer oven is fixed on the front top portion, which has an LED Screen displace along with all the program keys and adjustment keys. The Display screen indicates the ongoing operations and the timer when is food is the cooking side. It indicates when the device is switched ON/OFF when the device is ready to ADD food when to flip the food and the cooking time and temperature. In case of any error, the screen also indicates it on display.

Then there are these smart program keys that are present at the center of the control panel. There are separate keys for Air fryer, roast, bake, broil, reheat and dehydrate mode. When any of the keys are pressed the oven automatically adjusts its cooking temperature and time accordingly.

However, if you want to adjust the time and temperature manually, there are + and − keys for both time and temperature and you can use these keys to either increase or decrease the values respectively. Besides these keys, there are options to Start and Cancel a cooking function. There is key to switch ON/OFF the light inside the oven.

Inside The Oven:

There is a number of trays, baskets, and racks which are given with the oven to aid all types of cooking operations.

1. Drip pan: this pan is placed at the bottom of the oven to collect all the drippings from the food. The pan is removed after every session, and then it can be washed using soapy water or in the dish-washed.
2. Cooking trays: there are two cooking trays that come with this air fryer oven so that user can cook large servings in a single session.
3. Rotisserie spit and forks: this spit and fork set is used to hang the rotisserie chicken inside the Air fryer oven.
4. Rotisserie basket: This basket can be used for different functions. You can place rotisserie chicken inside it, or air fry other snacks and food items.
5. Rotisserie fetch tool: We know it is always difficult to remove the freshly cooked chicken from the rotisserie rod; therefore, the Instant Air fryer oven comes with a fetch tool to remove it easily.

How to Use the Instant Plus Vortex Air Fry Oven

Now that you know all the functions of the control panels and how it used. We shall see how you can put your Air fryer oven to better use. There are a few basic steps to start with that mainly includes the preparing of the device:

Prepare the Device:

- Start by checking all the components of the Instant Vortex Plus Air fryer oven and see if they in good shape and well instant, especially the power cord. Any fault in the power cord can be hazardous.
- Right after unboxing the device, it is important to clean the appliance inside out using a clean piece of cloth and wash all the removable accessories of the oven before the use.
- When everything is in place, plug in the device and press the power button to switch on the device.
- Set the dripping tray at the bottom of the oven and set the other accessories over it according to the use.

How to Cook:

When it comes to Instant Vortex oven, cooking becomes a piece of cake. Initially, it may take some time to develop the understanding of its functions and the relation of temperature with the cooking time, but with the variety of recipes shared in this cookbook, you will also get over that part easily. Here are some simple rules to cook a range of meals in the vortex oven:

1. At first, look for a suitable pan or utensil to add your food to the oven. Normally baking pans and trays are used for baking and other purposes whereas Air frying requires the basket and you may need rotisseries accessories to roast the whole chicken.
2. The device needs some time to preheat, so I would recommend not to add food before preheating. However, keep it ready aside while the device preheats.
3. Now select the desired cooking mode by pressing their respective buttons. When you press their buttons, the screen will display the default time and temperature.
4. To change the time and temperature, press the + or – keys accordingly. Then press the Start button.

5. At this point, the machine preheats to maintain the selected temperature. During this time, the timer does not start.
6. Once preheated, the LED screen will show the "ADD" food sign. Open the door and set the food inside.
7. Close the door again and press Start to resume cooking. Now the timer will start ticking, and you can also check the food by pressing the Light button.
8. If the food requires to be flipped or turned, then the appliance will automatically show the sign on display.
9. Open the door and turn or toss the food, then close it then the appliance will resume cooking.
10. The machine will beep when the timer goes off.
11. Remove the food from the oven and serve.

Cleaning and Maintenance

The Instant Plus Vortex Air Fry Oven is specially designed to give all its users an easy cleaning and smart maintenance.

1. When the cooking session is completed, unplug the oven and leave it on your countertop to cool down.
2. Once it is cooled completely, remove its removable door and clean it well with a wet cloth. Avoid scrubbing it hard.
3. Remove all the removable items from inside and wash then thoroughly using soap water. It is better to wash and dry them in your dishwasher.
4. In the interior of the oven can be cleaned with a slightly damp cloth. Simple wipe off the walls and remove all the grease and food particles, if any.
5. Use a dry cloth to wipe off the exterior of the oven.
6. Fix the oven door back into its place along with all the accessories, and the device is ready to use again.

Chapter 2: Breakfast Recipes

Nuts & Seeds Granola

Preparation Time: 15 minutes
Cooking Time: 15 minutes
Servings: 8

Ingredients:

- 1/3 cup olive oil
- ¼ cup maple syrup
- 2 tablespoons honey
- ½ teaspoon vanilla extract
- 2 cups rolled oats
- ½ cup wheat germ, toasted
- ¼ cup dried cherries
- ¼ cup dried blueberries
- 2 tablespoons dried cranberries
- 2 tablespoons sunflower seeds
- 2 tablespoons pumpkin seeds, shelled
- 1 tablespoon flax seed
- 2 tablespoons pecans, chopped
- 2 tablespoons hazelnuts, chopped
- 2 tablespoons almonds, chopped
- 2 tablespoons walnuts, chopped
- ½ teaspoon ground cinnamon
- 1/8 t teaspoon ground cloves

Method:

1. In a small bowl, add the oil and maple syrup and mix well.
2. In a large bowl, add the remaining ingredients and mix well.
3. Add the oil mixture and mix until well combined.
4. Place the mixture into a baking dish that will fit in the Vortex Plus Air Fryer Oven.
5. Select "Air Fry" and then adjust the temperature to 350 degrees F.
6. Set the timer for 15 minutes and press the "Start".

7. When the display shows "Add Food" insert the baking dish in the center position.
8. Stir the granola after every 5 minutes.
9. When cooking time is complete, remove the baking dish from oven.
10. Set the granola side to cool completely before serving.

Nutritional Information per Serving:

- Calories 302
- Total Fat 16.1 g
- Saturated Fat 2.1 g
- Cholesterol 0 mg
- Sodium 4 mg

- Total Carbs 35.1 g
- Fiber 5.7 g
- Sugar 14 g
- Protein 6.9 g

Simple Bagels

Preparation Time: 1 minutes
Cooking Time: 12 minutes
Servings: 4

Ingredients:

- 1 cup all-purpose flour
- 2 teaspoons baking powder
- Salt, to taste
- 1 cup plain Greek yogurt
- 1 egg, beaten
- 1 tablespoon water
- 1 tablespoon sesame seeds
- 1 teaspoon coarse salt

Method:

1. In a large bowl, mix together the flour, baking powder and salt.
2. Add the yogurt and mix until a dough ball forms.
3. Place the dough onto a lightly floured surface and then, cut into 4 equal-sized balls.
4. Roll each ball into a 7-8-inch rope and then join ends to shape a bagel.
5. Place 2 bagels onto each cooking tray.
6. In a small bowl, add egg and water and mix well.
7. Brush the bagels with egg mixture evenly.
8. Sprinkle the top with sesame seeds and salt, pressing lightly.
9. Arrange the drip pan in the bottom of Instant Vortex Plus Air Fryer Oven cooking chamber.
10. Select "Air Fry" and then adjust the temperature to 330 degrees F.
11. Set the timer for 12 minutes and press the "Start".
12. When the display shows "Add Food" insert the cooking trays in the center position and one tray in the top position.
13. When the display shows "Turn Food" do not turn the food but switch the position of cooking trays.
14. When cooking time is complete, remove the tray from oven.
15. Serve with your favorite topping.

Nutritional Information per Serving:

- Calories 188
- Total Fat 3.3 g
- Saturated Fat 1.2 g
- Cholesterol 45 mg
- Sodium 580mg
- Total Carbs 29.9 g
- Fiber 1.2 g
- Sugar 4.5 g
- Protein 8.5 g

Eggs & Cheese Puffs

Preparation Time: 1 minutes
Cooking Time: 20 minutes
Servings: 4

Ingredients:

- 1 (8-ounce) frozen puff pastry sheet, thawed
- ¾ cup Monterey Jack cheese, shredded and divided
- 4 large eggs
- 1 tablespoon fresh chives, minced

Method:

1. Unfold the puff pastry and arrange onto a lightly floured surface.
2. Cut pastry into 2 equal-sized squares.
3. Arrange 2 squares onto a cooking tray.
4. Arrange the drip pan in the bottom of Instant Vortex Plus Air Fryer Oven cooking chamber.
5. Select "Air Fry" and then adjust the temperature to 390 degrees F.
6. Set the timer for 10 minutes and press the "Start".
7. When the display shows "Add Food" insert the cooking tray in the center position.
8. After 5 minutes, remove the tray of pastry from the cooking chamber.
9. With a metal spoon, press down the center of each pastry to make a nest.
10. Place ¼ of the cheese into each nest and carefully, push it to the sides.
11. Carefully crack an egg into each nest and return the tray to the cooking chamber.
12. When the display shows "Turn Food" do nothing.
13. When cooking time is complete, remove the tray from oven.
14. Repeat with the remaining pastry squares, cheese and eggs.
15. Garnish with chives and serve warm.

Nutritional Information per Serving:

- Calories 398
- Total Fat 27.6 g
- Saturated Fat 7.8 g
- Cholesterol 186 mg
- Sodium 234 mg
- Total Carbs 26.2 g
- Fiber 0.9 g
- Sugar 0.8 g
- Protein 11.3 g

Egg, Bacon & Cheese Puffs

Preparation Time: 15 minutes
Cooking Time: 20 minutes
Servings: 4

Ingredients:

- 1 (8-ounce) frozen puff pastry sheet, thawed
- 2/3 cup cheddar cheese, shredded
- 4 cooked bacon slices, crumbled
- 4 eggs
- 1 tablespoon fresh parsley, chopped

Method:

1. Unfold the puff pastry and arrange onto a lightly floured surface.
2. Cut pastry into 2 equal-sized squares.
3. Arrange 2 squares onto a cooking tray.
4. Arrange the drip pan in the bottom of Instant Vortex Plus Air Fryer Oven cooking chamber.
5. Select "Air Fry" and then adjust the temperature to 390 degrees F.
6. Set the timer for 10 minutes and press the "Start".
7. When the display shows "Add Food" insert the cooking tray in the center position.
8. After 5 minutes, removed the tray of pastry from the cooking chamber.
9. With a metal spoon, press down the center of each pastry to make a nest.
10. Place ¼ of the cheese into each nest and carefully, push it to the sides.
11. Now, place ¼ of the bacon around the edges of the nest.
12. Carefully crack an egg into each nest and insert the tray to the cooking chamber.
13. When the display shows "Turn Food" do nothing.
14. When cooking time is complete, remove the tray from oven.
15. Repeat with the remaining pastry squares, cheese, bacon and eggs.
16. Garnish with parsley and serve warm.

Nutritional Information per Serving:

- Calories 608
- Total Fat 44.3 g
- Saturated Fat 14.8 g
- Cholesterol 215 mg
- Sodium 990 mg
- Total Carbs 26.6 g
- Fiber 0 g
- Sugar 0.9 g
- Protein 25.1 g

Breakfast Egg Rolls

Preparation Time: 20 minutes
Cooking Time: 11 minutes
Servings: 12

Ingredients:

- ½ pound bulk pork sausage
- ½ cup cheddar cheese, shredded
- ½ cup Monterrey Jack cheese, shredded
- 1 tablespoon scallion, chopped
- 4 large eggs
- 1 tablespoon 2% milk
- Salt and ground black pepper, as required
- 1 tablespoon butter
- 12 egg roll wrappers
- Olive oil cooking spray

Method:

1. Heat a small nonstick skillet over medium heat and cook the sausage for about 5-6 minutes, breaking into crumbles.
2. Drain the grease from skillet.
3. Stir in the cheeses and scallion and transfer the mixture into a bowl.
4. In a small bowl, add the eggs, milk, salt and black pepper and beat until well combined.
5. In another small skillet, melt the butter over medium heat.
6. Add the egg mixture and cook for about 2-3 minutes, stirring continuously.
7. Remove from the heat and stir with the sausage mixture.
8. Arrange 1 egg roll wrapper onto a smooth surface.
9. Place ¼ cup of filling over one corner of a wrapper, just below the center.
10. Fold the bottom corner over filling.
11. With wet fingers, moisten the remaining wrapper edges.
12. Fold side corners toward center over filling.
13. Roll egg roll up tightly and with your fingers, press at tip to seal.
14. Repeat with the remaining wrappers and filling.
15. Arrange the 6 rolls onto a cooking tray and spray with the cooking spray.

16. Arrange the drip pan in the bottom of Instant Vortex Plus Air Fryer Oven cooking chamber.
17. Select "Air Fry" and then adjust the temperature to 400 degrees F.
18. Set the timer for 8 minutes and press the "Start".
19. When the display shows "Add Food" insert the cooking tray in the center position.
20. When the display shows "Turn Food" turn the rolls and spray with the cooking spray.
21. Repeat with the remaining wrappers ad filling.
22. Serve warm.

Nutritional Information per Serving:

- Calories 212
- Total Fat 10.3 g
- Saturated Fat 4.1 g
- Cholesterol 88 mg
- Sodium 401 mg
- Total Carbs 18.9 g
- Fiber 0.6 g
- Sugar 0.2 g
- Protein 10.3 g

Veggies Frittata

Preparation Time: 15 minutes
Cooking Time: 15 minutes
Servings: 4

Ingredients:

- 4 eggs
- 3 tablespoons heavy cream
- Salt, as required
- 4 tablespoons Cheddar cheese, grated
- 4 fresh mushrooms, sliced
- 4 tablespoons fresh spinach, chopped
- 3 grape tomatoes, halved
- 2 tablespoons fresh mixed herbs, chopped
- 1 scallion, sliced

Method:

1. In a bowl, add the eggs, cream and salt and beat well.
2. Add the remaining ingredients and stir to combine.
3. Place the mixture into a greased pan evenly.
4. Arrange the drip pan in the bottom of Instant Vortex Plus Air Fryer Oven cooking chamber.
5. Select "Air Fry" and then adjust the temperature to 350 degrees F.
6. Set the timer for 15 minutes and press the "Start".
7. When the display shows "Add Food" place the baking pan over the drip pan.
8. When the display shows "Turn Food" do nothing.
9. When cooking time is complete, remove the pan from Vortex and serve warm.

Nutritional Information per Serving:

- Calories 139
- Total Fat 11 g
- Saturated Fat 5.4 g
- Cholesterol 187 mg
- Sodium 152 mg
- Total Carbs 2.4 g
- Fiber 0.7 g
- Sugar 1 g
- Protein 8.4 g

Eggs in Bread Hole

Preparation Time: 10 minutes
Cooking Time: 6 minutes
Servings: 2

Ingredients:

- 2 whole-wheat bread slices
- 2 large eggs
- Salt and ground black pepper, as required

Method:

1. Arrange the drip pan in the bottom of Instant Vortex Plus Air Fryer Oven cooking chamber.
2. Select "Air Fry" and then adjust the temperature to 320 degrees F.
3. Set the timer for 6 minutes and press the "Start".
4. With a cookie cutter, cut a hole in the center of each bread slice.
5. Arrange the bread slices in the cooking tray.
6. Crack 1 egg in the hole of each bread slice.
7. When the display shows "Add Food" insert the cooking tray in the center position.
8. When cooking time is complete, remove the tray from oven.
9. Sprinkle the top of egg with salt and black pepper and serve.

Nutritional Information per Serving:

- Calories 141
- Total Fat 5.9 g
- Saturated Fat 1.8 g
- Cholesterol 186 mg
- Sodium 280 mg
- Total Carbs 12 g
- Fiber 1.9 g
- Sugar 2 g
- Protein 9.9 g

French Toast Sticks

Preparation Time: 10 minutes
Cooking Time: 10 minutes
Servings: 2

Ingredients:

- 2 bread slices
- 2 tablespoons milk
- ½ tablespoon butter, melted
- 1 small egg, beaten
- 1 tablespoon sugar
- ¼ teaspoon ground cinnamon
- ½ teaspoon vanilla extract

Method:

1. Cut each slice of bread into 3 strip pieces.
2. In a bowl, add the remaining ingredients and mix well.
3. Dip each bread stick in egg mixture.
4. Arrange the drip pan in the bottom of Instant Vortex Plus Air Fryer Oven cooking chamber.
5. Select "Air Fry" and then adjust the temperature to 370 degrees F.
6. Set the timer for 10 minutes and press the "Start".
7. Arrange the bread sticks onto the lightly greased cooking tray.
8. When the display shows "Add Food" insert the cooking tray in the center position.
9. When the display shows "Turn Food" turn the bread sticks.
10. When cooking time is complete, remove the tray from oven.
11. Serve warm.

Nutritional Information per Serving:

- Calories 110
- Total Fat 5.3 g
- Saturated Fat 2.6 g
- Cholesterol 78 mg
- Sodium 115 mg
- Total Carbs 11.8 g
- Fiber 0.4 g
- Sugar 7.4 g
- Protein 3.6 g

Sausage & Bacon Omelet

Preparation Time: 10 minutes
Cooking Time: 10 minutes
Servings: 2

Ingredients:

- 4 eggs
- Ground black pepper, as required
- 1 bacon slice, chopped
- 2 sausages, chopped
- 1 onion, chopped
- 1 teaspoon fresh parsley, minced

Method:

1. In a bowl, crack the eggs and black pepper and beat well.
2. Add the remaining ingredients and gently, stir to combine.
3. Place the mixture into a baking pan.
4. Arrange the drip pan in the bottom of Instant Vortex Plus Air Fryer Oven cooking chamber.
5. Select "Air Fry" and then adjust the temperature to 320 degrees F.
6. Set the timer for 10 minutes and press the "Start".
7. When the display shows "Add Food" place the baking pan over the drip pan.
8. When the display shows "Turn Food" do nothing.
9. When cooking time is complete, remove the pan from Vortex and serve warm.

Nutritional Information per Serving:

- Calories 508
- Total Fat 38.4 g
- Saturated Fat 12.3 g
- Cholesterol 413 mg
- Sodium 1000 mg
- Total Carbs 6.1 g
- Fiber 1.2 g
- Sugar 3 g
- Protein 33.2 g

Sausage with Eggs

Preparation Time: 10 minutes
Cooking Time: 6 minutes
Servings: 2

Ingredients:

- 4 breakfast sausage
- 2 hard-boiled eggs, peeled
- 1 avocado, peeled, pitted and sliced

Method:

1. Arrange the sausages in the rotisserie basket and attach the lid.
2. Arrange the drip pan in the bottom of Instant Vortex Plus Air Fryer Oven cooking chamber.
3. Select "Roast" and then adjust the temperature to 375 degrees F.
4. Set the timer for 6 minutes and press the "Start".
5. When the display shows "Add Food" arrange the rotisserie basket, on the rotisserie spit.
6. Then, close the door and touch "Rotate".
7. When cooking time is complete, press the red lever to release the rod.
8. Remove from the Vortex and place the sausages onto serving plates.
9. Divide eggs and avocado slices onto each plate and serve.

Nutritional Information per Serving:

- Calories 322
- Total Fat 28.5 g
- Saturated Fat 6.9 g
- Cholesterol 177 mg
- Sodium 187 mg
- Total Carbs 9 g
- Fiber 6.7 g
- Sugar 0.8 g
- Protein 10.6 g

Chapter 3: Poultry Recipes

Roasted Spicy Chicken

Preparation Time: 10 minutes
Cooking Time: 40 minutes
Servings: 4

Ingredients:

- 1 teaspoon dried oregano
- 1 teaspoon dried rosemary
- 1 teaspoon paprika
- 1 teaspoon garlic powder
- Salt and ground black pepper, as required
- 1 (3-pound) whole chicken, neck and giblets removed
- 1 lemon, quartered
- 3 garlic cloves, halved
- 2 fresh rosemary sprigs
- 2 tablespoons olive oil

Method:

1. In a small bowl, mix together the dried herbs, spices, salt and black pepper.
2. Stuff the chicken cavity with lemon, garlic, and rosemary sprigs.
3. With kitchen twine, tie the chicken.
4. Coat the chicken with oil evenly and then, rub with the herb mixture.
5. Insert the rotisserie rod through the chicken.
6. Insert the rotisserie forks, one on each side of the rod to secure the rod to the chicken.
7. Arrange the drip pan in the bottom of Instant Vortex Plus Air Fryer Oven cooking chamber.
8. Select "Roast" and then adjust the temperature to 375 degrees F.
9. Set the timer for 40 minutes and press the "Start".
10. When the display shows "Add Food" press the red lever down and load the left side of the rod into the Vortex.
11. Now, slide the rod's left side into the groove along the metal bar so it doesn't move.
12. Then, close the door and touch "Rotate".

13. When cooking time is complete, press the red lever to release the rod.
14. Remove from the Vortex and place the chicken onto a platter for about 5-10 minutes before carving.
15. With a sharp knife, cut the chicken into desired sized pieces and serve.

Nutritional Information per Serving:

- Calories 584
- Total Fat 17.5 g
- Saturated Fat 3.9 g
- Cholesterol 262 mg
- Sodium 254 mg

- Total Carbs 2.3 g
- Fiber 0.7 g
- Sugar 0.4 g
- Protein 99 g

Spicy Chicken Legs

Preparation Time: 15 minutes
Cooking Time: 25 minutes
Servings: 6

Ingredients:

- 2½ pounds chicken legs
- 2 tablespoons olive oil
- 1 teaspoon smoked paprika
- 1 teaspoon garlic powder
- ½ teaspoon ground cumin
- Salt and ground black pepper, as required

Method:

1. In a large bowl, add all the ingredients and mix well.
2. Arrange the chicken legs onto 2 cooking trays evenly.
3. Arrange the drip pan in the bottom of Instant Vortex Plus Air Fryer Oven cooking chamber.
4. Select "Air Fry" and then adjust the temperature to 400 degrees F.
5. Set the timer for 25 minutes and press the "Start".
6. When the display shows "Add Food" insert 1 tray in the top position and another in the bottom position.
7. When the display shows "Turn Food" do not turn the food but switch the position of cooking trays.
8. When cooking time is complete, remove the trays from Vortex.
9. Serve hot.

Nutritional Information per Serving:

- Calories 402
- Total Fat 18.8 g
- Saturated Fat 4.5 g
- Cholesterol 168 mg
- Sodium 190 mg
- Total Carbs 0.6 g
- Fiber 0.2 g
- Sugar 0.2 g
- Protein 54.8 g

Spiced Chicken Thighs

Preparation Time: 15 minutes
Cooking Time: 20 minutes
Servings: 4

Ingredients:

- 1 teaspoon ground cumin
- 1 teaspoon garlic powder
- ½ teaspoon smoked paprika
- ½ teaspoon ground coriander
- Salt and ground black pepper, as required
- 4 (5-ounce) chicken thighs
- 2 tablespoons olive oil

Method:

1. In a large bowl, add the spices, salt and black pepper and mix well.
2. Coat the chicken thighs with oil and then, rub with spice mixture.
3. Arrange the chicken thighs onto the cooking tray.
4. Arrange the drip pan in the bottom of Instant Vortex Plus Air Fryer Oven cooking chamber.
5. Select "Air Fry" and then adjust the temperature to 400 degrees F.
6. Set the timer for 20 minutes and press the "Start".
7. When the display shows "Add Food" insert the cooking tray in the center position.
8. When the display shows "Turn Food" turn the chicken thighs.
9. When cooking time is complete, remove the chicken pieces.
10. Serve hot.

Nutritional Information per Serving:

- Calories 334
- Total Fat 17.7 g
- Saturated Fat 3.9 g
- Cholesterol 126 mg
- Sodium 162 mg
- Total Carbs 0.9 g
- Fiber 0.2g
- Sugar 0.2 g
- Protein 41.3 g

Breaded Chicken Breasts

Preparation Time: 15 minutes
Cooking Time: 12 minutes
Servings: 6

Ingredients:

- 1 cup breadcrumbs
- ½ cup Parmesan cheese, grated
- ¼ cup fresh parsley, minced
- Salt and ground black pepper, as required
- 1½ pounds boneless, skinless chicken breasts
- 3 tablespoons olive oil
- Olive oil cooking spray

Method:

1. In a shallow dish, add the breadcrumbs, Parmesan cheese, parsley, salt and black pepper mix well.
2. Rub the chicken breasts with oil and then, coat with the breadcrumb's mixture evenly.
3. Arrange the chicken breasts onto the cooking tray and spray with cooking spray.
4. Arrange the drip pan in the bottom of Instant Vortex Plus Air Fryer Oven cooking chamber.
5. Select "Air Fry" and then adjust the temperature to 350 degrees F.
6. Set the timer for 12 minutes and press the "Start".
7. When the display shows "Add Food" insert the cooking tray in the center position.
8. When the display shows "Turn Food" turn the chicken breasts.
9. When cooking time is complete, remove the chicken breasts.
10. Serve hot.

Nutritional Information per Serving:

- Calories 371
- Total Fat 18 g
- Saturated Fat 4.3 g
- Cholesterol 106 mg
- Sodium 315 mg
- Total Carbs 13.1 g
- Fiber 0.9 g
- Sugar 1.1 g
- Protein 38 g

BBQ Chicken Wings

Preparation Time: 20 minutes
Cooking Time: 25 minutes
Servings: 4

Ingredients:

- 2 pounds chicken wingettes and drumettes
- ½ cup ketchup
- 3 tablespoons white vinegar
- 2 tablespoons honey
- 2 tablespoons molasses
- ½ teaspoon liquid smoke
- ¼ teaspoon paprika
- ¼ teaspoon garlic powder
- Pinch of cayenne pepper

Method:

1. Arrange the wings onto 2 cooking trays in a single layer.
2. Arrange the drip pan in the bottom of Instant Vortex Plus Air Fryer Oven cooking chamber.
3. Select "Air Fry" and then adjust the temperature to 380 degrees F.
4. Set the timer for 25 minutes and press the "Start".
5. When the display shows "Add Food" insert 1 tray in the top position and another in the bottom position.
6. When the display shows "Turn Food" do not turn the food but switch the position of cooking trays.
7. Meanwhile, in a small pan, add the remaining ingredients over medium heat and cook for about 10 minutes, stirring occasionally.
8. When cooking time is complete, remove the trays from Vortex.
9. In a large bowl, add the chicken wings and honey mixture and toss to coat well.
10. Serve immediately.

Nutritional Information per Serving:

- Calories 524
- Total Fat 16.9 g
- Saturated Fat 4.6 g
- Cholesterol 202 mg

- Sodium 534 mg
- Total Carbs 24 g
- Fiber 0.2 g

- Sugar 21.1 g
- Protein 66.2 g

Simple Turkey Breast

Preparation Time: 10 minutes
Cooking Time: 45 minutes
Servings: 8

Ingredients:

- 1 (3-pound) turkey breast
- Salt and ground black pepper, as required

Method:

1. Season the turkey breast with salt and black pepper evenly.
2. With kitchen twines, tie the turkey breast to keep it compact.
3. Arrange the turkey breast in the rotisserie basket and attach the lid.
4. Arrange the drip pan in the bottom of Instant Vortex Plus Air Fryer Oven cooking chamber.
5. Select "Air Fry" and then adjust the temperature to 360 degrees F.
6. Set the timer for 45 minutes and press the "Start".
7. Then, Then, close the door and touch "Rotate".
8. When the display shows "Add Food" arrange the rotisserie basket, on the rotisserie spit.
9. Then, close the door and touch "Rotate".
10. When cooking time is complete, press the red lever to release the rod.
11. Remove from the Vortex and place the turkey breast onto a platter for about 5-10 minutes before slicing.
12. With a sharp knife, cut the turkey breast into desired sized slices and serve.

Nutritional Information per Serving:

- Calories 153
- Total Fat 1.5 g
- Saturated Fat 0 g
- Cholesterol 61 mg
- Sodium 500 mg
- Total Carbs 3 g
- Fiber 0 g
- Sugar 3 g
- Protein 31.9 g

Herbed Turkey Breast

Preparation Time: 15 minutes
Cooking Time: 1 hour
Servings: 8

Ingredients:

- 2 tablespoons olive oil
- 2 tablespoons lemon juice
- 1 tablespoon garlic, minced
- 2 teaspoons ground mustard
- Salt and ground black pepper, as required
- 1 teaspoon ground sage
- 1 teaspoon dried thyme
- 1 teaspoon dried rosemary
- 1 (3-pound) turkey breast

Method:

1. In a small bowl, add all the ingredients except the turkey breast and mix until well combined.
2. Rub the oil mixture on the outside of the turkey breast and under any loose skin generously.
3. Arrange the turkey breast onto a cooking tray, skin side up.
4. Arrange the drip pan in the bottom of Instant Vortex Plus Air Fryer Oven cooking chamber.
5. Select "Air Fry" and then adjust the temperature to 360 degrees F.
6. Set the timer for 60 minutes and press the "Start".
7. When the display shows "Add Food" insert the cooking tray in the center position.
8. When cooking time is complete, press the red lever to release the rod.
9. Remove from the Vortex and place the turkey breast onto a platter for about 5-10 minutes before slicing.
10. With a sharp knife, cut the turkey breast into desired sized slices and serve.

Nutritional Information per Serving:

- Calories 214
- Total Fat 6.6 g
- Saturated Fat 1.1 g
- Cholesterol 73 mg

- Sodium 800 mg
- Total Carbs 8.1 g
- Fiber 1.2 g

- Sugar 6.1 g
- Protein 29.4 g

Chapter 4: Meat Recipes

Simple Beef Sirloin Roast

Preparation Time: 10 minutes
Cooking Time: 50 minutes
Servings: 8

Ingredients:

- 2½ pounds sirloin roast
- Salt and ground black pepper, as required

Method:

1. Rub the roast with salt and black pepper generously.
2. Insert the rotisserie rod through the roast.
3. Insert the rotisserie forks, one on each side of the rod to secure the rod to the chicken.
4. Arrange the drip pan in the bottom of Instant Vortex Plus Air Fryer Oven cooking chamber.
5. Select "Roast" and then adjust the temperature to 350 degrees F.
6. Set the timer for 50 minutes and press the "Start".
7. When the display shows "Add Food" press the red lever down and load the left side of the rod into the Vortex.
8. Now, slide the rod's left side into the groove along the metal bar so it doesn't move.
9. Then, close the door and touch "Rotate".
10. When cooking time is complete, press the red lever to release the rod.
11. Remove from the Vortex and place the roast onto a platter for about 10 minutes before slicing.
12. With a sharp knife, cut the roast into desired sized slices and serve.

Nutritional Information per Serving:

- Calories 201
- Total Fat 8.8 g
- Saturated Fat 3.1 g
- Cholesterol 94 mg
- Sodium 88 mg
- Total Carbs 0 g
- Fiber 0 g
- Sugar 0 g
- Protein 28.9 g

Seasoned Beef Roast

Preparation Time: 10 minutes
Cooking Time: 45 minutes
Servings: 10

Ingredients:

- 3 pounds beef top roast
- 1 tablespoon olive oil
- 2 tablespoons Montreal steak seasoning

Method:

1. Coat the roast with oil and then rub with the seasoning generously.
2. With kitchen twines, tie the roast to keep it compact.
3. Arrange the roast onto the cooking tray.
4. Arrange the drip pan in the bottom of Instant Vortex Plus Air Fryer Oven cooking chamber.
5. Select "Air Fry" and then adjust the temperature to 360 degrees F.
6. Set the timer for 45 minutes and press the "Start".
7. When the display shows "Add Food" insert the cooking tray in the center position.
8. When the display shows "Turn Food" do nothing.
9. When cooking time is complete, remove the tray from Vortex and place the roast onto a platter for about 10 minutes before slicing.
10. With a sharp knife, cut the roast into desired sized slices and serve.

Nutritional Information per Serving:

- Calories 269
- Total Fat 9.9 g
- Saturated Fat 3.4 g
- Cholesterol 122 mg
- Sodium 538 mg
- Total Carbs 0 g
- Fiber 0 g
- Sugar 0 g
- Protein 41.3 g

Bacon Wrapped Filet Mignon

Preparation Time: 10 minutes
Cooking Time: 15 minutes
Servings: 2

Ingredients:

- 2 bacon slices
- 2 (4-ounce) filet mignon
- Salt and ground black pepper, as required
- Olive oil cooking spray

Method:

1. Wrap 1 bacon slice around each filet mignon and secure with toothpicks.
2. Season the filets with the salt and black pepper lightly.
3. Arrange the filet mignon onto a coking rack and spray with cooking spray.
4. Arrange the drip pan in the bottom of Instant Vortex Plus Air Fryer Oven cooking chamber.
5. Select "Air Fry" and then adjust the temperature to 375 degrees F.
6. Set the timer for 15 minutes and press the "Start".
7. When the display shows "Add Food" insert the cooking rack in the center position.
8. When the display shows "Turn Food" turn the filets.
9. When cooking time is complete, remove the rack from Vortex and serve hot.

Nutritional Information per Serving:

- Calories 360
- Total Fat 19.6 g
- Saturated Fat 6.8 g
- Cholesterol 108 mg
- Sodium 737 mg
- Total Carbs 0.4 g
- Fiber 0 g
- Sugar 0 g
- Protein 42.6 g

Beef Burgers

Preparation Time: 15 minutes
Cooking Time: 18 minutes
Servings: 4

Ingredients:

For Burgers:

- 1 pound ground beef
- ½ cup panko breadcrumbs
- ¼ cup onion, chopped finely
- 3 tablespoons Dijon mustard
- 3 teaspoons low-sodium soy sauce
- 2 teaspoons fresh rosemary, chopped finely
- Salt, to taste

For Topping:

- 2 tablespoons Dijon mustard
- 1 tablespoon brown sugar
- 1 teaspoon soy sauce
- 4 Gruyere cheese slices

Method:

1. In a large bowl, add all the ingredients and mix until well combined.
2. Make 4 equal-sized patties from the mixture.
3. Arrange the patties onto a cooking tray.
4. Arrange the drip pan in the bottom of Instant Vortex Plus Air Fryer Oven cooking chamber.
5. Select "Air Fry" and then adjust the temperature to 370 degrees F.
6. Set the timer for 15 minutes and press the "Start".
7. When the display shows "Add Food" insert the cooking rack in the center position.
8. When the display shows "Turn Food" turn the burgers.
9. Meanwhile, for sauce: in a small bowl, add the mustard, brown sugar and soy sauce and mix well.

10. When cooking time is complete, remove the tray from Vortex and coat the burgers with the sauce.
11. Top each burger with 1 cheese slice.
12. Return the tray to the cooking chamber and select "Broil".
13. Set the timer for 3 minutes and press the "Start".
14. When cooking time is complete, remove the tray from Vortex and serve hot.

Nutritional Information per Serving:

- Calories 402
- Total Fat 18 g
- Saturated Fat 8.5 g
- Cholesterol 133mg
- Sodium 651 mg
- Total Carbs 6.3 g
- Fiber 0.8 g
- Sugar 3 g
- Protein 44.4 g

Beef Jerky

Preparation Time: 15 minutes
Cooking Time: 3 hours
Servings: 4

Ingredients:

- 1½ pounds beef round, trimmed
- ½ cup Worcestershire sauce
- ½ cup low-sodium soy sauce
- 2 teaspoons honey
- 1 teaspoon liquid smoke
- 2 teaspoons onion powder
- ½ teaspoon red pepper flakes
- Ground black pepper, as required

Method:

1. In a zip-top bag, place the beef and freeze for 1-2 hours to firm up.
2. Place the meat onto a cutting board and cut against the grain into 1/8-¼-inch strips.
3. In a large bowl, add the remaining ingredients and mix until well combined.
4. Add the steak slices and coat with the mixture generously.
5. Refrigerate to marinate for about 4-6 hours.
6. Remove the beef slices from bowl and with paper towels, pat dry them.
7. Divide the steak strips onto the cooking trays and arrange in an even layer.
8. Select "Dehydrate" and then adjust the temperature to 160 degrees F.
9. Set the timer for 3 hours and press the "Start".
10. When the display shows "Add Food" insert 1 tray in the top position and another in the center position.
11. After 1½ hours, switch the position of cooking trays.
12. Meanwhile, in a small pan, add the remaining ingredients over medium heat and cook for about 10 minutes, stirring occasionally.
13. When cooking time is complete, remove the trays from Vortex.

Nutritional Information per Serving:

- Calories 372
- Total Fat 10.7 g

- Saturated Fat 4 g
- Cholesterol 152 mg
- Sodium 2000 mg
- Total Carbs 12 g

- Fiber 0.2 g
- Sugar 11.3 g
- Protein 53.8 g

Sweet & Spicy Meatballs

Preparation Time: 20 minutes
Cooking Time: 30 minutes
Servings: 8

Ingredients:

For Meatballs:

- 2 pounds lean ground beef
- 2/3 cup quick-cooking oats
- ½ cup Ritz crackers, crushed
- 1 (5-ounce) can evaporated milk
- 2 large eggs, beaten lightly
- 1 teaspoon honey
- 1 tablespoon dried onion, minced
- 1 teaspoon garlic powder
- 1 teaspoon ground cumin
- Salt and ground black pepper, as required

For Sauce:

- 1/3 cup orange marmalade
- 1/3 cup honey
- 1/3 cup brown sugar
- 2 tablespoons cornstarch
- 2 tablespoons soy sauce
- 1-2 tablespoons hot sauce
- 1 tablespoon Worcestershire sauce

Method:

1. For meatballs: in a large bowl, add all the ingredients and mix until well combined.
2. Make 1½-inch balls from the mixture.
3. Arrange half of the meatballs onto a cooking tray in a single layer.
4. Arrange the drip pan in the bottom of Instant Vortex Plus Air Fryer Oven cooking chamber.
5. Select "Air Fry" and then adjust the temperature to 380 degrees F.

6. Set the timer for 15 minutes and press the "Start".
7. When the display shows "Add Food" insert the cooking tray in the center position.
8. When the display shows "Turn Food" turn the meatballs.
9. When cooking time is complete, remove the tray from Vortex.
10. Repeat with the remaining meatballs.
11. Meanwhile, for sauce: in a small pan, add all the ingredients over medium heat and cook until thickened, stirring continuously.
12. . Serve the meatballs with the topping of sauce.

Nutritional Information per Serving:

- Calories 411
- Total Fat 11.1 g
- Saturated Fat 4.1 g
- Cholesterol 153 mg
- Sodium 448 mg

- Total Carbs 38.8 g
- Fiber 1 g
- Sugar 28.1 g
- Protein 38.9 g

Spiced Pork Shoulder

Preparation Time: 15 minutes
Cooking Time: 55 minutes
Servings: 6

Ingredients:

- 1 teaspoon ground cumin
- 1 teaspoon cayenne pepper
- 1 teaspoon garlic powder
- Salt and ground black pepper, as required
- 2 pounds skin-on pork shoulder

Method:

1. In a small bowl, mix together the spices, salt and black pepper.
2. Arrange the pork shoulder onto a cutting board, skin-side down.
3. Season the inner side of pork shoulder with salt and black pepper.
4. With kitchen twines, tie the pork shoulder into a long round cylinder shape.
5. Season the outer side of pork shoulder with spice mixture.
6. Insert the rotisserie rod through the pork shoulder.
7. Insert the rotisserie forks, one on each side of the rod to secure the pork shoulder.
8. Arrange the drip pan in the bottom of Instant Vortex Plus Air Fryer Oven cooking chamber.
9. Select "Roast" and then adjust the temperature to 350 degrees F.
10. Set the timer for 55 minutes and press the "Start".
11. When the display shows "Add Food" press the red lever down and load the left side of the rod into the Vortex.
12. Now, slide the rod's left side into the groove along the metal bar so it doesn't move.
13. Then, close the door and touch "Rotate".
14. When cooking time is complete, press the red lever to release the rod.
15. Remove the pork from Vortex and place onto a platter for about 10 minutes before slicing.
16. With a sharp knife, cut the pork shoulder into desired sized slices and serve.

Nutritional Information per Serving:

- Calories 445
- Total Fat 32.5 g

- Saturated Fat 11.9 g
- Cholesterol 136 mg
- Sodium 131 mg
- Total Carbs 0.7 g

- Fiber 0.2 g
- Sugar 0.2 g
- Protein 35.4 g

Seasoned Pork Tenderloin

Preparation Time: 10 minutes
Cooking Time: 45 minutes
Servings: 5

Ingredients:

- 1½ pounds pork tenderloin
- 2-3 tablespoons BBQ pork seasoning

Method:

1. Rub the pork with seasoning generously.
2. Insert the rotisserie rod through the pork tenderloin.
3. Insert the rotisserie forks, one on each side of the rod to secure the pork tenderloin.
4. Arrange the drip pan in the bottom of Instant Vortex Plus Air Fryer Oven cooking chamber.
5. Select "Roast" and then adjust the temperature to 360 degrees F.
6. Set the timer for 45 minutes and press the "Start".
7. When the display shows "Add Food" press the red lever down and load the left side of the rod into the Vortex.
8. Now, slide the rod's left side into the groove along the metal bar so it doesn't move.
9. Then, close the door and touch "Rotate".
10. When cooking time is complete, press the red lever to release the rod.
11. Remove the pork from Vortex and place onto a platter for about 10 minutes before slicing.
12. With a sharp knife, cut the roast into desired sized slices and serve.

Nutritional Information per Serving:

- Calories 195
- Total Fat 4.8 g
- Saturated Fat 1.6 g
- Cholesterol 99 mg
- Sodium 116 mg
- Total Carbs 0 g
- Fiber 0 g
- Sugar 0 g
- Protein 35.6 g

Garlicky Pork Tenderloin

Preparation Time: 15 minutes
Cooking Time: 20 minutes
Servings: 5

Ingredients:

- 1½ pounds pork tenderloin
- Nonstick cooking spray
- 2 small heads roasted garlic
- Salt and ground black pepper, as required

Method:

1. Lightly, spray all the sides of pork with cooking spray and then, season with salt and black pepper.
2. Now, rub the pork with roasted garlic.
3. Arrange the roast onto the lightly greased cooking tray.
4. Arrange the drip pan in the bottom of Instant Vortex Plus Air Fryer Oven cooking chamber.
5. Select "Air Fry" and then adjust the temperature to 400 degrees F.
6. Set the timer for 20 minutes and press the "Start".
7. When the display shows "Add Food" insert the cooking tray in the center position.
8. When the display shows "Turn Food" turn the pork.
9. When cooking time is complete, remove the tray from Vortex and place the roast onto a platter for about 10 minutes before slicing.
10. With a sharp knife, cut the roast into desired sized slices and serve.

Nutritional Information per Serving:

- Calories 202
- Total Fat 4.8 g
- Saturated Fat 1.6 g
- Cholesterol 99 mg
- Sodium 109 mg
- Total Carbs 1.7 g
- Fiber 0.1 g
- Sugar 0.1 g
- Protein 35.9 g

Glazed Pork Tenderloin

Preparation Time: 15 minutes
Cooking Time: 20 minutes
Servings: 3

Ingredients:

- 1 pound pork tenderloin
- 2 tablespoons Sriracha
- 2 tablespoons honey
- Salt, as required

Method:

1. Insert the rotisserie rod through the pork tenderloin.
2. Insert the rotisserie forks, one on each side of the rod to secure the pork tenderloin.
3. In a small bowl, add the Sriracha, honey and salt and mix well.
4. Brush the pork tenderloin with honey mixture evenly.
5. Arrange the drip pan in the bottom of Instant Vortex Plus Air Fryer Oven cooking chamber.
6. Select "Air Fry" and then adjust the temperature to 350 degrees F.
7. Set the timer for 20 minutes and press the "Start".
8. When the display shows "Add Food" press the red lever down and load the left side of the rod into the Vortex.
9. Now, slide the rod's left side into the groove along the metal bar so it doesn't move.
10. Then, close the door and touch "Rotate".
11. When cooking time is complete, press the red lever to release the rod.
12. Remove the pork from Vortex and place onto a platter for about 10 minutes before slicing.
13. With a sharp knife, cut the roast into desired sized slices and serve.

Nutritional Information per Serving:

- Calories 269
- Total Fat 5.3 g
- Saturated Fat 1.8 g
- Cholesterol 110 mg
- Sodium 207 mg
- Total Carbs 13.5 g
- Fiber 0 g
- Sugar 11.6 g
- Protein 39.7 g

Honey Mustard Pork Tenderloin

Preparation Time: 15 minutes
Cooking Time: 25 minutes
Servings: 3

Ingredients:

- 1 pound pork tenderloin
- 1 tablespoon garlic, minced
- 2 tablespoons soy sauce
- 2 tablespoons honey
- 1 tablespoon Dijon mustard
- 1 tablespoon grain mustard
- 1 teaspoon Sriracha sauce

Method:

1. In a large bowl, add all the ingredients except pork and mix well.
2. Add the pork tenderloin and coat with the mixture generously.
3. Refrigerate to marinate for 2-3 hours.
4. Remove the pork tenderloin from bowl, reserving the marinade.
5. Place the pork tenderloin onto the lightly greased cooking tray.
6. Arrange the drip pan in the bottom of Instant Vortex Plus Air Fryer Oven cooking chamber.
7. Select "Air Fry" and then adjust the temperature to 380 degrees F.
8. Set the timer for 25 minutes and press the "Start".
9. When the display shows "Add Food" insert the cooking tray in the center position.
10. When the display shows "Turn Food" turn the pork and oat with the reserved marinade.
11. When cooking time is complete, remove the tray from Vortex and place the pork tenderloin onto a platter for about 10 minutes before slicing.
12. With a sharp knife, cut the pork tenderloin into desired sized slices and serve.

Nutritional Information per Serving:

- Calories 277
- Total Fat 5.7 g
- Saturated Fat 1.8 g
- Cholesterol 110 mg
- Sodium 782 mg
- Total Carbs 14.2 g
- Fiber 0.4 g
- Sugar 11.8 g
- Protein 40.7 g

Seasoned Pork Chops

Preparation Time: 10 minutes
Cooking Time: 12 minutes
Servings: 4

Ingredients:

- 4 (6-ounce) boneless pork chops
- 2 tablespoons pork rub
- 1 tablespoon olive oil

Method:

1. Coat both sides of the pork chops with the oil and then, rub with the pork rub.
2. Place the pork chops onto the lightly greased cooking tray.
3. Arrange the drip pan in the bottom of Instant Vortex Plus Air Fryer Oven cooking chamber.
4. Select "Air Fry" and then adjust the temperature to 400 degrees F.
5. Set the timer for 12 minutes and press the "Start".
6. When the display shows "Add Food" insert the cooking tray in the center position.
7. When the display shows "Turn Food" turn the pork chops.
8. When cooking time is complete, remove the tray from Vortex and serve hot.

Nutritional Information per Serving:

- Calories 285
- Total Fat 9.5 g
- Saturated Fat 2.5 g
- Cholesterol 124 mg
- Sodium 262 mg
- Total Carbs 1.5 g
- Fiber 0 g
- Sugar 0.8 g
- Protein 44.5 g

Breaded Pork Chops

Preparation Time: 15 minutes
Cooking Time: 28 minutes
Servings: 2

Ingredients:

- 2 (5-ounce) boneless pork chops
- 1 cup buttermilk
- ½ cup flour
- 1 teaspoon garlic powder
- Salt and ground black pepper, as required
- Olive oil cooking spray

Method:

1. In a bowl, place the chops and buttermilk and refrigerate, covered for about 12 hours.
2. Remove the chops from the bowl of buttermilk, discarding the buttermilk.
3. In a shallow dish, mix together the flour, garlic powder, salt, and black pepper.
4. Coat the chops with flour mixture generously.
5. Place the pork chops onto the cooking tray and spray with the cooking spray.
6. Arrange the drip pan in the bottom of Instant Vortex Plus Air Fryer Oven cooking chamber.
7. Select "Air Fry" and then adjust the temperature to 380 degrees F.
8. Set the timer for 28 minutes and press the "Start".
9. When the display shows "Add Food" insert the cooking tray in the center position.
10. When the display shows "Turn Food" turn the pork chops.
11. When cooking time is complete, remove the tray from Vortex and serve hot.

Nutritional Information per Serving:

- Calories 370
- Total Fat 6.4 g
- Saturated Fat 2.4 g
- Cholesterol 108 mg
- Sodium 288 mg
- Total Carbs 30.7 g
- Fiber 1 g
- Sugar 6.3 g
- Protein 44.6 g

Crusted Rack of Lamb

Preparation Time: 15 minutes
Cooking Time: 19 minutes
Servings: 4

Ingredients:

- 1 rack of lamb, trimmed all fat and frenched
- Salt and ground black pepper, as required
- 1/3 cup pistachios, chopped finely
- 2 tablespoons panko breadcrumbs
- 2 teaspoons fresh thyme, chopped finely
- 1 teaspoon fresh rosemary, chopped finely
- 1 tablespoon butter, melted
- 1 tablespoon Dijon mustard

Method:

1. Insert the rotisserie rod through the rack on the meaty side of the ribs, right next to the bone.
2. Insert the rotisserie forks, one on each side of the rod to secure the rack.
3. Season the rack with salt and black pepper evenly.
4. Arrange the drip pan in the bottom of Instant Vortex Plus Air Fryer Oven cooking chamber.
5. Select "Air Fry" and then adjust the temperature to 380 degrees F.
6. Set the timer for 12 minutes and press the "Start".
7. When the display shows "Add Food" press the red lever down and load the left side of the rod into the Vortex.
8. Now, slide the rod's left side into the groove along the metal bar so it doesn't move.
9. Then, close the door and touch "Rotate".
10. Meanwhile, in a small bowl, mix together the remaining ingredients except the mustard.
11. When cooking time is complete, press the red lever to release the rod.
12. Remove the rack from Vortex and brush the meaty side with the mustard.
13. Then, coat the pistachio mixture on all sides of the rack and press firmly.
14. Now, place the rack of lamb onto the cooking tray, meat side up.
15. Select "Air Fry" and adjust the temperature to 380 degrees F.

16. Set the timer for 7 minutes and press the "Start".
17. When the display shows "Add Food" insert the cooking tray in the center position.
18. When the display shows "Turn Food" do nothing.
19. When cooking time is complete, remove the tray from Vortex and place the rack onto a cutting board for at least 10 minutes.
20. Cut the rack into individual chops and serve.

Nutritional Information per Serving:

- Calories 824
- Total Fat 39.3 g
- Saturated Fat 14.2 g
- Cholesterol 233 mg
- Sodium 373 mg
- Total Carbs 10.3 g
- Fiber 1.2 g
- Sugar 0.2 g
- Protein 72 g

Lamb Burgers

Preparation Time: 15 minutes
Cooking Time: 8 minutes
Servings: 6

Ingredients:

- 2 pounds ground lamb
- 1 tablespoon onion powder
- Salt and ground black pepper, as required

Method:

1. In a bowl, add all the ingredients and mix well.
2. Make 6 equal-sized patties from the mixture.
3. Arrange the patties onto a cooking tray.
4. Arrange the drip pan in the bottom of Instant Vortex Plus Air Fryer Oven cooking chamber.
5. Select "Air Fry" and then adjust the temperature to 360 degrees F.
6. Set the timer for 8 minutes and press the "Start".
7. When the display shows "Add Food" insert the cooking rack in the center position.
8. When the display shows "Turn Food" turn the burgers.
9. When cooking time is complete, remove the tray from Vortex and serve hot.

Nutritional Information per Serving:

- Calories 285
- Total Fat 11.1 g
- Saturated Fat 4 g
- Cholesterol 136 mg
- Sodium 143 mg
- Total Carbs 0.9 g
- Fiber 0.1 g
- Sugar 0.4 g
- Protein 42.6 g

Chapter 5: Fish & Seafood Recipes

Lemony Salmon

Preparation Time: 15 minutes
Cooking Time: 10 minutes
Servings: 2

Ingredients:

- 1 tablespoon fresh lemon juice
- ½ tablespoons olive oil
- Salt and ground black pepper, as required
- 1 garlic clove, minced
- ½ teaspoon fresh thyme leaves, chopped
- 2 (7-ounce) salmon fillets

Method:

1. In a bowl, add all the ingredients except the salmon and mix well.
2. Add the salmon fillets and coat with the mixture generously.
3. Coat the fillets with flour mixture, then dip into egg mixture and finally coat with the cornflake mixture.
4. Arrange the salmon fillets onto a lightly greased cooking rack, skin-side down.
5. Arrange the drip pan in the bottom of Instant Vortex Plus Air Fryer Oven cooking chamber.
6. Select "Air Fry" and then adjust the temperature to 400 degrees F.
7. Set the timer for 10 minutes and press the "Start".
8. When the display shows "Add Food" insert the cooking rack in the bottom position.
9. When the display shows "Turn Food" turn the fillets.
10. When cooking time is complete, remove the tray from Vortex and serve hot.

Nutritional Information per Serving:

- Calories 297
- Total Fat 15.8 g
- Saturated Fat 2.3 g
- Cholesterol 88 mg
- Sodium 167 mg
- Total Carbs 0.8 g
- Fiber 0.2 g
- Sugar 0.2 g
- Protein 38.7 g

Breaded Cod

Preparation Time: 15 minutes
Cooking Time: 10 minutes
Servings: 4

Ingredients:

- 1/3 cup all-purpose flour
- Ground black pepper, as required
- 1 large egg
- 2 tablespoons water
- 2/3 cup cornflakes, crushed
- 1 tablespoon Parmesan cheese, grated
- 1/8 teaspoon cayenne pepper
- 1 pound cod fillets
- Salt, as required

Method:

1. Put the flour and black pepper in a shallow dish and mix well.
2. In a second shallow dish, add the egg and water and beat well.
3. In a third shallow dish, add the cornflakes, cheese and cayenne pepper. and mix well.
4. Season the cod fillets with salt evenly.
5. Coat the fillets with flour mixture, then dip into egg mixture and finally coat with the cornflake mixture.
6. Arrange the cod fillets onto a cooking tray.
7. Arrange the drip pan in the bottom of Instant Vortex Plus Air Fryer Oven cooking chamber.
8. Select "Air Fry" and then adjust the temperature to 400 degrees F.
9. Set the timer for 10 minutes and press the "Start".
10. When the display shows "Add Food" insert the cooking rack in the bottom position.
11. When the display shows "Turn Food" turn the cod fillets.
12. When cooking time is complete, remove the tray from Vortex and serve hot.

Nutritional Information per Serving:

- Calories 168
- Total Fat 2.7 g
- Saturated Fat 0.6 g
- Cholesterol 103 mg
- Sodium 172 mg

- Total Carbs 12.1 g
- Fiber 0.5g
- Sugar 0.6 g
- Protein 23.7 g

Crispy Haddock

Preparation Time: 15 minutes
Cooking Time: 10 minutes
Servings: 3

Ingredients:

- ½ cup flour
- ½ teaspoon paprika
- 1 egg beaten
- ¼ cup mayonnaise
- 4 ounces salt and vinegar potato chips, crushed finely
- 1 pound haddock fillet, cut into 6 pieces

Method:

1. In a shallow dish, mix together the flour and paprika.
2. In a second shallow dish, add the egg and mayonnaise and beat well.
3. In a third shallow dish, place the crushed potato chips.
4. Coat the fish pieces with flour mixture, then dip into egg mixture and finally coat with the potato chips.
5. Arrange the fish pieces onto 2 cooking trays.
6. Arrange the drip pan in the bottom of Instant Vortex Plus Air Fryer Oven cooking chamber.
7. Select "Air Fry" and then adjust the temperature to 370 degrees F.
8. Set the timer for 10 minutes and press the "Start".
9. When the display shows "Add Food" insert 1 cooking tray in the top position and another in the bottom position.
10. When the display shows "Turn Food" do not turn the food but switch the position of cooking trays.
11. When cooking time is complete, remove the trays from Vortex and serve hot.

Nutritional Information per Serving:

- Calories 546
- Total Fat 22.7 g
- Saturated Fat 5.8 g
- Cholesterol 172 mg
- Sodium 295 mg
- Total Carbs 40.9 g
- Fiber 2.5 g
- Sugar 1.5 g
- Protein 43.5 g

Spiced Tilapia

Preparation Time: 15 minutes
Cooking Time: 12 minutes
Servings: 2

Ingredients:

- ½ teaspoon lemon pepper seasoning
- ½ teaspoon garlic powder
- 1/2 teaspoon onion powder
- Salt and ground black pepper, as required
- 2 (6-ounce) tilapia fillets
- 1 tablespoon olive oil

Method:

1. In a small bowl, mix together the spices, salt and black pepper.
2. Coat the tilapia fillets with oil and then rub with spice mixture.
3. Arrange the salmon fillets onto a lightly greased cooking rack, skin-side down.
4. Arrange the drip pan in the bottom of Instant Vortex Plus Air Fryer Oven cooking chamber.
5. Select "Air Fry" and then adjust the temperature to 360 degrees F.
6. Set the timer for 12 minutes and press the "Start".
7. When the display shows "Add Food" insert the cooking rack in the bottom position.
8. When the display shows "Turn Food" turn the fillets.
9. When cooking time is complete, remove the tray from Vortex and serve hot.

Nutritional Information per Serving:

- Calories 206
- Total Fat 8.6 g
- Saturated Fat 1.7 g
- Cholesterol 83 mg
- Sodium 138 mg
- Total Carbs 0.2 g
- Fiber 0.2 g
- Sugar 0.4 g
- Protein 31.9 g

Tuna Burgers

Preparation Time: 15 minutes
Cooking Time: 6 minutes
Servings: 4

Ingredients:

- 7 ounces canned tuna
- 1 large egg
- ¼ cup breadcrumbs
- 1 tablespoon mustard
- ¼ teaspoon garlic powder
- ¼ teaspoon onion powder
- ¼ teaspoon cayenne pepper
- Salt and ground black pepper, as required

Method:

1. In a bowl, add all the ingredients and mix until well combined.
2. Make 4 equal-sized patties from the mixture.
3. Arrange the patties onto a cooking tray.
4. Arrange the drip pan in the bottom of Instant Vortex Plus Air Fryer Oven cooking chamber.
5. Select "Air Fry" and then adjust the temperature to 400 degrees F.
6. Set the timer for 6 minutes and press the "Start".
7. When the display shows "Add Food" insert the cooking rack in the center position.
8. When the display shows "Turn Food" turn the burgers.
9. When cooking time is complete, remove the tray from Vortex and serve hot.

Nutritional Information per Serving:

- Calories 151
- Total Fat 6.4 g
- Saturated Fat 1.3 g
- Cholesterol 62 mg
- Sodium 131 mg
- Total Carbs 6.3 g
- Fiber 0.8 g
- Sugar 0.8 g
- Protein 16.4 g

Crispy Shrimp

Preparation Time: 20 minutes
Cooking Time: 12 minutes
Servings: 4

Ingredients:

- ½ cup all-purpose flour
- Salt and ground white pepper, as required
- 2 egg whites
- ¾ cup plain breadcrumbs
- ½ cup unsweetened coconut, shredded
- 2 teaspoons lime zest, grated finely
- 1 pound shrimp, peeled and deveined

Method:

1. In a shallow dish, add the flour, salt and white pepper and mix well.
2. In a second shallow dish, add the egg whites and beat lightly.
3. In a third shallow dish, mix together the breadcrumbs, coconut and lime zest.
4. Coat the shrimp with flour mixture, then dip into egg whites and finally coat with the coconut mixture.
5. Arrange the coated shrimp onto 2 cooking trays in a single layer.
6. Arrange the drip pan in the bottom of Instant Vortex Plus Air Fryer Oven cooking chamber.
7. Select "Air Fry" and then adjust the temperature to 400 degrees F.
8. Set the timer for 12 minutes and press the "Start".
9. When the display shows "Add Food" insert 1 tray in the top position and another in the bottom position.
10. When the display shows "Turn Food" do not turn the food but switch the position of cooking trays.
11. When cooking time is complete, remove the trays from Vortex and serve hot.

Nutritional Information per Serving:

- Calories 316
- Total Fat 6.5 g
- Saturated Fat 3.8 g
- Cholesterol 318 mg
- Sodium 642 mg
- Total Carbs 30 g
- Fiber 2.3 g
- Sugar 2.1 g
- Protein 32.3 g

Lemony Shrimp

Preparation Time: 15 minutes
Cooking Time: 8 minutes
Servings: 3

Ingredients:

- 2 tablespoons fresh lemon juice
- 1 tablespoon olive oil
- 1 teaspoon lemon pepper
- ¼ teaspoon paprika
- ¼ teaspoon garlic powder
- 12 ounces medium shrimp, peeled and deveined

Method:

1. In a large bowl, add all the ingredients except the shrimp and mix until well combined.
2. Add the shrimp and toss to coat well.
3. Arrange the shrimps onto a cooking tray.
4. Arrange the drip pan in the bottom of Instant Vortex Plus Air Fryer Oven cooking chamber.
5. Select "Air Fry" and then adjust the temperature to 400 degrees F.
6. Set the timer for 8 minutes and press the "Start".
7. When the display shows "Add Food" insert the cooking rack in the center position.
8. When the display shows "Turn Food" o nothing.
9. When cooking time is complete, remove the tray from Vortex and serve hot.

Nutritional Information per Serving:

- Calories 154
- Total Fat 6.1 g
- Saturated Fat 0.8 g
- Cholesterol 2230 mg
- Sodium 259 mg
- Total Carbs 0.9 g
- Fiber 0.3 g
- Sugar 0.3 g
- Protein 24.5 g

Crab Cakes

Preparation Time: 15 minutes
Cooking Time: 10 minutes
Servings: 4

Ingredients:

- ¼ cup red bell pepper, seeded and chopped finely
- 2 scallions, chopped finely
- 2 tablespoons mayonnaise
- 2 tablespoons breadcrumbs
- 1 tablespoon Dijon mustard
- 1 teaspoon old bay seasoning
- 8 ounces lump crabmeat, drained

Method:

1. In a large bowl, add all the ingredients except crabmeat and mix until well combined.
2. Gently fold in the crabmeat.
3. Make 4 equal-sized patties from the mixture.
4. Arrange the patties onto a lightly greased cooking tray.
5. Arrange the drip pan in the bottom of Instant Vortex Plus Air Fryer Oven cooking chamber.
6. Select "Air Fry" and then adjust the temperature to 370 degrees F.
7. Set the timer for 10 minutes and press the "Start".
8. When the display shows "Add Food" insert the cooking rack in the center position.
9. When the display shows "Turn Food" do nothing.
10. When cooking time is complete, remove the tray from Vortex and serve hot.

Nutritional Information per Serving:

- Calories 91
- Total Fat 7.4 g
- Saturated Fat 0.4 g
- Cholesterol 34 mg
- Sodium 603 mg
- Total Carbs 6.4 g
- Fiber 0.6 g
- Sugar 1.3 g
- Protein 9.1 g

Chapter 6: Vegetarian Recipes

Seasoned Potatoes

Preparation Time: 10 minutes
Cooking Time: 40 minutes
Servings: 2

Ingredients:

- 2 russet potatoes, scrubbed
- ½ tablespoon butter, melted
- ½ teaspoon garlic & herb blend seasoning
- ½ teaspoon garlic powder
- Salt, to taste

Method:

1. In a small bowl, mix together the spices and salt.
2. With a fork, prick the potatoes.
3. Coat the potatoes with butter and sprinkle with spice mixture.
4. Arrange the potatoes onto a cooking tray.
5. Arrange the drip pan in the bottom of Instant Vortex Plus Air Fryer Oven cooking chamber.
6. Select "Air Fry" and then adjust the temperature to 400 degrees F.
7. Set the timer for 40 minutes and press the "Start".
8. When the display shows "Add Food" insert the cooking rack in the center position.
9. When the display shows "Turn Food" do nothing.
10. When cooking time is complete, remove the tray from Vortex and serve hot.

Nutritional Information per Serving:

- Calories 176
- Total Fat 2.1 g
- Saturated Fat 1.9 g
- Cholesterol 8 mg
- Sodium 111 mg
- Total Carbs 34.2 g
- Fiber 5.2 g
- Sugar 2.6 g
- Protein 3.8 g

Thyme Potatoes

Preparation Time: 15 minutes
Cooking Time: 20 minutes
Servings: 4

Ingredients:

- 1 pound small red potatoes, cut into 1-inch pieces
- 1 tablespoon olive oil
- 2 teaspoons fresh thyme, chopped
- Salt and ground black pepper, as required
- 1 tablespoon lemon zest, grated

Method:

1. In a bowl, add all the ingredients except lemon zest and toss to coat well.
2. Place the potatoes in the rotisserie basket and attach the lid.
3. Arrange the drip pan in the bottom of Instant Vortex Plus Air Fryer Oven cooking chamber.
4. Select "Air Fry" and then adjust the temperature to 400 degrees F.
5. Set the timer for 20 minutes and press the "Start".
6. Then, close the door and touch "Rotate".
7. When the display shows "Add Food" arrange the rotisserie basket, on the rotisserie spit.
8. Then, close the door and touch "Rotate".
9. When cooking time is complete, press the red lever to release the rod.
10. Remove from the Vortex and transfer the potatoes into a bowl.
11. Add the lemon zest and toss to coat well.
12. Serve immediately.

Nutritional Information per Serving:

- Calories 112
- Total Fat 3.7 g
- Saturated Fat 0.6 g
- Cholesterol 0 mg
- Sodium 46 mg
- Total Carbs 18.7 g
- Fiber 2.2 g
- Sugar 1.2 g
- Protein 2.2 g

Parmesan Broccoli

Preparation Time: 10 minutes
Cooking Time: 6 minutes
Servings: 4

Ingredients:

- 1 pound small broccoli florets
- 1 tablespoon garlic, minced
- 2 tablespoons olive oil
- ¼ cup Parmesan cheese, grated

Method:

1. In a bowl, add all the ingredients and toss to coat well.
2. Arrange the broccoli florets onto a cooking tray.
3. Arrange the drip pan in the bottom of Instant Vortex Plus Air Fryer Oven cooking chamber.
4. Select "Air Fry" and then adjust the temperature to 350 degrees F.
5. Set the timer for 6 minutes and press the "Start".
6. When the display shows "Add Food" insert the cooking tray in the center position.
7. When the display shows "Turn Food" turn the broccoli florets.
8. When cooking time is complete, remove the tray from Vortex and serve hot.

Nutritional Information per Serving:

- Calories 112
- Total Fat 3.7 g
- Saturated Fat 0.6 g
- Cholesterol 0 mg
- Sodium 46 mg
- Total Carbs 18.7 g
- Fiber 2.2 g
- Sugar 1.2 g
- Protein 2.2 g

Buttered Cauliflower

Preparation Time: 15 minutes
Cooking Time: 15 minutes
Servings: 4

Ingredients:

- 1 pound cauliflower head, cut into florets
- 1 tablespoon butter, melted
- ½ teaspoon red pepper flakes, crushed
- Salt and ground black pepper, as required

Method:

1. In a bowl, add all the ingredients and toss to coat well.
2. Place the potatoes in the rotisserie basket and attach the lid.
3. Arrange the drip pan in the bottom of Instant Vortex Plus Air Fryer Oven cooking chamber.
4. Select "Air Fry" and then adjust the temperature to 400 degrees F.
5. Set the timer for 15 minutes and press the "Start".
6. Then, close the door and touch "Rotate".
7. When the display shows "Add Food" arrange the rotisserie basket, on the rotisserie spit.
8. Then, close the door and touch "Rotate".
9. When cooking time is complete, press the red lever to release the rod.
10. Remove from the Vortex and serve immediately.

Nutritional Information per Serving:

- Calories 55
- Total Fat 3 g
- Saturated Fat 1.9 g
- Cholesterol 8 mg
- Sodium 93 mg
- Total Carbs 6.1 g
- Fiber 2.9 g
- Sugar 2.7 g
- Protein 2.3 g

Simple Asparagus

Preparation Time: 10 minutes
Cooking Time: 10 minutes
Servings: 3

Ingredients:

- 1 pound fresh thick asparagus, trimmed
- 1 tablespoon olive oil
- Salt and ground black pepper, as required

Method:

1. In a bowl, add all the ingredients and toss to coat well.
2. Arrange the asparagus onto a cooking tray.
3. Arrange the drip pan in the bottom of Instant Vortex Plus Air Fryer Oven cooking chamber.
4. Select "Air Fry" and then adjust the temperature to 350 degrees F.
5. Set the timer for 10 minutes and press the "Start".
6. When the display shows "Add Food" insert the cooking tray in the center position.
7. When the display shows "Turn Food" turn the asparagus.
8. When cooking time is complete, remove the tray from Vortex and serve hot.

Nutritional Information per Serving:

- Calories 70
- Total Fat 4.9 g
- Saturated Fat 0.7 g
- Cholesterol 0 mg
- Sodium 53 mg
- Total Carbs 5.9 g
- Fiber 3.2 g
- Sugar 2.8 g
- Protein 3.3 g

Vinegar Brussels Sprout

Preparation Time: 15 minutes
Cooking Time: 20 minutes
Servings: 4

Ingredients:

- 1 pound Brussels Sprouts, ends trimmed and cut into bite-sized pieces
- 1 tablespoon balsamic vinegar
- 1 tablespoon olive oil
- Salt and ground black pepper, as required

Method:

1. In a bowl, add all the ingredients and toss to coat well.
2. Place the Brussels Sprout in the rotisserie basket and attach the lid.
3. Arrange the drip pan in the bottom of Instant Vortex Plus Air Fryer Oven cooking chamber.
4. Select "Air Fry" and then adjust the temperature to 350 degrees F.
5. Set the timer for 20 minutes and press the "Start".
6. Then, close the door and touch "Rotate".
7. When the display shows "Add Food" arrange the rotisserie basket, on the rotisserie spit.
8. Then, close the door and touch "Rotate".
9. When cooking time is complete, press the red lever to release the rod.
10. Remove from the Vortex and serve hot.

Nutritional Information per Serving:

- Calories 80
- Total Fat 3.9 g
- Saturated Fat 0.6 g
- Cholesterol 0 mg
- Sodium 67 mg
- Total Carbs 10.3 g
- Fiber 4.3 g
- Sugar 2.5 g
- Protein 3.9 g

Spiced Zucchini

Preparation Time: 10 minutes
Cooking Time: 12 minutes
Servings: 3

Ingredients:

- 1 pound zucchini, cut into ½-inch thick slices lengthwise
- 1 tablespoon olive oil
- ½ teaspoon garlic powder
- ½ teaspoon cayenne pepper
- Salt and ground black pepper, as required

Method:

1. In a bowl, add all the ingredients and toss to coat well.
2. Arrange the zucchini slices onto a cooking tray.
3. Arrange the drip pan in the bottom of Instant Vortex Plus Air Fryer Oven cooking chamber.
4. Select "Air Fry" and then adjust the temperature to 400 degrees F.
5. Set the timer for 12 minutes and press the "Start".
6. When the display shows "Add Food" insert the cooking tray in the center position.
7. When the display shows "Turn Food" do nothing.
8. When cooking time is complete, remove the tray from Vortex and serve hot.

Nutritional Information per Serving:

- Calories 67
- Total Fat 5 g
- Saturated Fat 0.7 g
- Cholesterol 0 mg
- Sodium 66 mg
- Total Carbs 5.6 g
- Fiber 1.8 g
- Sugar 2.8 g
- Protein 2 g

Green Beans with Carrots

Preparation Time: 15 minutes
Cooking Time: 10 minutes
Servings: 3

Ingredients:

- ½ pound green beans, trimmed
- ½ pound carrots, peeled and cut into sticks
- 1 tablespoon olive oil
- Salt and ground black pepper, as required

Method:

1. In a bowl, add all the ingredients and toss to coat well.
2. Place the vegetables in the rotisserie basket and attach the lid.
3. Arrange the drip pan in the bottom of Instant Vortex Plus Air Fryer Oven cooking chamber.
4. Select "Air Fry" and then adjust the temperature to 400 degrees F.
5. Set the timer for 10 minutes and press the "Start".
6. Then, close the door and touch "Rotate".
7. When the display shows "Add Food" arrange the rotisserie basket, on the rotisserie spit.
8. Then, close the door and touch "Rotate".
9. When cooking time is complete, press the red lever to release the rod.
10. Remove from the Vortex and serve.

Nutritional Information per Serving:

- Calories 94
- Total Fat 4.8 g
- Saturated Fat 0.7 g
- Cholesterol 0 mg
- Sodium 107 mg
- Total Carbs 12.7 g
- Fiber 4.4 g
- Sugar 4.8 g
- Protein 2 g

Mixed Veggies Combo

Preparation Time: 15 minutes
Cooking Time: 12 minutes
Servings: 4

Ingredients:

- 1 cup baby carrots
- 1 cup broccoli florets
- 1 cup cauliflower florets
- 1 tablespoon olive oil
- 1 tablespoon Italian seasoning
- Salt and ground black pepper, as required

Method:

1. In a bowl, add all the ingredients and toss to coat well.
2. Place the vegetables in the rotisserie basket and attach the lid.
3. Arrange the drip pan in the bottom of Instant Vortex Plus Air Fryer Oven cooking chamber.
4. Select "Air Fry" and then adjust the temperature to 380 degrees F.
5. Set the timer for 18 minutes and press the "Start".
6. Then, close the door and touch "Rotate".
7. When the display shows "Add Food" arrange the rotisserie basket, on the rotisserie spit.
8. Then, close the door and touch "Rotate".
9. When cooking time is complete, press the red lever to release the rod.
10. Remove from the Vortex and serve.

Nutritional Information per Serving:

- Calories 66
- Total Fat 4.7 g
- Saturated Fat 0.7 g
- Cholesterol 2 mg
- Sodium 74 mg
- Total Carbs 5.7 g
- Fiber 1.9 g
- Sugar 2.7 g
- Protein 1.4 g

Chapter 7: Snacks & Appetizer Recipes

Cauliflower Popcorns

Preparation Time: 15 minutes
Cooking Time: 12 hours
Servings: 4

Ingredients:

- 2 pounds head cauliflower, cut into small florets
- 2 tablespoons hot sauce
- 1 tablespoon fresh lime juice
- 1 tablespoon oil
- 1 tablespoon smoked paprika
- 1 teaspoon ground cumin

Method:

1. In a bowl, add all the ingredients and toss to coat well.
2. Arrange the cauliflower florets onto 2 cooking trays.
3. Arrange the drip pan in the bottom of Instant Vortex Plus Air Fryer Oven cooking chamber.
4. Select "Dehydrate" and then adjust the temperature to 130 degrees F.
5. Set the timer for 12 hours and press the "Start".
6. When the display shows "Add Food" insert 1 tray in the top position and another in the bottom position.
7. When the display shows "Turn Food" do not turn the food but switch the position of cooking trays.
8. When cooking time is complete, remove the trays from Vortex and serve hot.

Nutritional Information per Serving:

- Calories 95
- Total Fat 4 g
- Saturated Fat 0.5 g
- Cholesterol 0 mg
- Sodium 260 mg
- Total Carbs 13.4 g
- Fiber 6.4 g
- Sugar 5.7 g
- Protein 4.9 g

Kale Chips

Preparation Time: 15 minutes
Cooking Time: 7 minutes
Servings: 4

Ingredients:

- 1 (8-ounce) bunch curly kale, tough ribs removed and torn into 2-inch pieces
- 1 tablespoon olive oil
- 1 teaspoon salt

Method:

1. In a large bowl, add all the ingredients and with your hands, massage the oil and salt into kale completely.
2. Arrange the kale pieces onto 2 cooking trays.
3. Arrange the drip pan in the bottom of Instant Vortex Plus Air Fryer Oven cooking chamber.
4. Select "Air Fry" and then adjust the temperature to 340 degrees F.
5. Set the timer for 7 minutes and press the "Start".
6. When the display shows "Add Food" insert 1 tray in the top position and another in the bottom position.
7. When the display shows "Turn Food" do not turn the food but switch the position of cooking trays.
8. When cooking time is complete, remove the trays from Vortex and transfer the kale chips into a bowl.
9. Serve hot.

Nutritional Information per Serving:

- Calories 58
- Total Fat 3.5 g
- Saturated Fat 0.5 g
- Cholesterol 0 mg
- Sodium 606 mg
- Total Carbs 5.9 g
- Fiber 0.9 g
- Sugar 0 g
- Protein 1.7 g

Potato Fries

Preparation Time: 15 minutes
Cooking Time: 16 minutes
Servings: 2

Ingredients:

- ½ pound potatoes, peeled and cut into ½-inch thick sticks lengthwise
- 1 tablespoon olive oil
- Salt and ground black pepper, as required

Method:

1. In a large bowl, add all the ingredients and toss to coat well.
2. Arrange the potato sticks onto a cooking tray.
3. Arrange the drip pan in the bottom of Instant Vortex Plus Air Fryer Oven cooking chamber.
4. Select "Air Fry" and then adjust the temperature to 400 degrees F.
5. Set the timer for 16 minutes and press the "Start".
6. When the display shows "Add Food" insert the cooking tray in the center position.
7. When the display shows "Turn Food" turn the potato sticks.
8. When cooking time is complete, remove the tray from Vortex and serve warm.

Nutritional Information per Serving:

- Calories 138
- Total Fat 7.1 g
- Saturated Fat 1 g
- Cholesterol 0 mg
- Sodium 84 mg
- Total Carbs 17.8 g
- Fiber 2.7 g
- Sugar 1.3 g
- Protein 1.9 g

Onion Rings

Preparation Time: 15 minutes
Cooking Time: 8 minutes
Servings: 4

Ingredients:

- 1 large onion, cut into ½-inch thick rings
- 3 tablespoons coconut flour
- Salt, as required
- 2 large eggs
- 2/3 cup pork rinds
- 3 tablespoons blanched almond flour
- ½ teaspoon paprika
- ½ teaspoon garlic powder

Method:

1. In a shallow dish, mix together the coconut flour and salt.
2. In a second shallow dish, add the eggs and beat lightly.
3. In a third shallow dish, mix together the pork rinds, almond flour and spices.
4. Coat the onion rings with flour mixture, then dip into egg whites and finally coat with the pork rind mixture.
5. Arrange the coated onion rings onto 2 lightly greased cooking trays in a single layer.
6. Arrange the drip pan in the bottom of Instant Vortex Plus Air Fryer Oven cooking chamber.
7. Select "Air Fry" and then adjust the temperature to 400 degrees F.
8. Set the timer for 8 minutes and press the "Start".
9. When the display shows "Add Food" insert 1 tray in the top position and another in the bottom position.
10. When the display shows "Turn Food" do not turn the food but switch the position of cooking trays.
11. When cooking time is complete, remove the trays from Vortex and serve hot.

Nutritional Information per Serving:

- Calories 180
- Total Fat 10.2 g
- Saturated Fat 3.2 g
- Cholesterol 111 mg

- Sodium 323 mg
- Total Carbs 9 g
- Fiber 3.7 g

- Sugar 1.9 g
- Protein 13.7 g

Crispy Pickle Slices

Preparation Time: 15 minutes
Cooking Time: 18 minutes
Servings: 8

Ingredients:

- 16 dill pickle slices
- ¼ cup all-purpose flour
- Salt, as required
- 2 small eggs, beaten lightly
- 1 tablespoon dill pickle juice
- ¼ teaspoon garlic powder
- ¼ teaspoon cayenne pepper
- 1 cup panko breadcrumbs
- 1 tablespoon fresh dill, minced
- Cooking spray

Method:

1. Place the pickle slices over paper towels for about 15 minutes or until all the liquid is absorbed.
2. Meanwhile, in a shallow dish, mix together the flour and salt.
3. In another shallow dish, add the eggs, pickle juice, garlic powder and cayenne and beat until well combined.
4. In a third shallow dish, mix together the panko and dill.
5. Coat the pickle slices with flour mixture, then dip into egg mixture and finally coat with the panko mixture.
6. Spray the pickle slices with cooking spray.
7. Arrange the pickle slices onto a cooking tray.
8. Arrange the drip pan in the bottom of Instant Vortex Plus Air Fryer Oven cooking chamber.
9. Select "Air Fry" and then adjust the temperature to 400 degrees F.
10. Set the timer for 18 minutes and press the "Start".
11. When the display shows "Add Food" insert the cooking tray in the center position.
12. When the display shows "Turn Food" turn the pickle slices.
13. When cooking time is complete, remove the tray from Vortex and serve warm.

Nutritional Information per Serving:

- Calories 80
- Total Fat 2 g
- Saturated Fat 0.7 g
- Cholesterol 34 mg
- Sodium 407 mg

- Total Carbs 6 g
- Fiber 0.4 g
- Sugar 0.3 g
- Protein 2.1 g

Beef Taquitos

Preparation Time: 15 minutes
Cooking Time: 8 minutes
Servings: 6

Ingredients:

- 6 corn tortillas
- 2 cups cooked beef, shredded
- ½ cup onion, chopped
- 1 cup pepper jack cheese, shredded
- Olive oil cooking spray

Method:

1. Arrange the tortillas onto a smooth surface.
2. Place the shredded meat over one corner of each tortilla, followed by onion and cheese.
3. Roll each tortilla to secure the filling and secure with toothpicks.
4. Spray each taquito with cooking spray evenly.
5. Arrange the taquitos onto a cooking tray.
6. Arrange the drip pan in the bottom of Instant Vortex Plus Air Fryer Oven cooking chamber.
7. Select "Air Fry" and then adjust the temperature to 400 degrees F.
8. Set the timer for 8 minutes and press the "Start".
9. When the display shows "Add Food" insert the cooking tray in the center position.
10. When the display shows "Turn Food" turn the taquitos.
11. When cooking time is complete, remove the tray from Vortex and serve warm.

Nutritional Information per Serving:

- Calories 263
- Total Fat 10.7 g
- Saturated Fat 5.2 g
- Cholesterol 84 mg
- Sodium 248 mg
- Total Carbs 12.3 g
- Fiber 1.7 g
- Sugar 0.6 g
- Protein 28.4 g

Cheese Sandwich

Preparation Time: 10 minutes
Cooking Time: 10 minutes
Servings: 2

Ingredients:

- 3 tablespoons butter, softened
- 4 white bread slices
- 2 cheddar cheese slices

Method:

1. Spread the butter over each bread slice generously.
2. Place 2 bread slices onto a cooking tray, buttered side down
3. Top each buttered bread slice with 1 cheese slice.
4. Cover with the remaining bread slices, buttered side up.
5. Arrange the sandwiches onto a cooking tray.
6. Arrange the drip pan in the bottom of Instant Vortex Plus Air Fryer Oven cooking chamber.
7. Select "Air Fry" and then adjust the temperature to 375 degrees F.
8. Set the timer for 10 minutes and press the "Start".
9. When the display shows "Add Food" insert the cooking tray in the center position.
10. When the display shows "Turn Food" turn the sandwiches.
11. When cooking time is complete, remove the tray from Vortex.
12. Cut each sandwich in half vertically and serve warm.

Nutritional Information per Serving:

- Calories 307
- Total Fat 27.2 g
- Saturated Fat 16.4 g
- Cholesterol 72 mg
- Sodium 425 mg
- Total Carbs 9.4 g
- Fiber 0.4 g
- Sugar 0.8 g
- Protein 8.2 g

Roasted Chickpeas

Preparation Time: 10 minutes
Cooking Time: 17 minutes
Servings: 6

Ingredients:

- 1 (15-ounce) can chickpeas, rinsed, drained and pat dried
- 1 teaspoon olive oil
- 1 tablespoon dry ranch seasoning mix

Method:

1. Place the chickpeas onto a cooking tray and spread in an even layer.
2. Arrange the drip pan in the bottom of Instant Vortex Plus Air Fryer Oven cooking chamber.
3. Insert the cooking tray in the center position.
4. Select "Air Fry" and then adjust the temperature to 390 degrees F.
5. Set the timer for 17 minutes and press the "Start".
6. When the display shows "Turn Food" turn the sandwiches.
7. When the display shows "Add Food" remove the chickpeas.
8. Drizzle the chickpeas with oil and toss to coat well.
9. Return the cooking tray to the cooking chamber.
10. When the display shows "Turn Food" stir the chickpeas.
11. When cooking time is complete, remove the tray from Vortex and transfer the chickpeas into a bowl.
12. Add the ranch seasoning and toss to coat well.
13. Serve cold.

Nutritional Information per Serving:

- Calories 268
- Total Fat 5.1 g
- Saturated Fat 0.6 g
- Cholesterol 0 mg
- Sodium 197 mg
- Total Carbs 43 g
- Fiber 12.3 g
- Sugar 7.6 g
- Protein 13.7 g

Chapter 8: Dessert Recipes

Apple Pie Rolls

Preparation Time: 20 minutes
Cooking Time: 12 minutes
Servings: 4

Ingredients:

- 1½ cups tart apples, peeled, cored and chopped
- ¼ cup light brown sugar
- 1¼ teaspoons ground cinnamon, divided
- ½ teaspoon corn starch
- 4 egg roll wrappers
- ¼ cup cream cheese, softened
- Olive oil cooking spray
- 1 tablespoon sugar

Method:

1. In a small bowl, mix together the apples, brown sugar, 1 teaspoon of cinnamon and corn starch.
2. Arrange 1 egg roll wrapper onto a smooth surface.
3. Spread about 1 tablespoon of cream cheese over roll, leaving 1-inch of edges.
4. Place 1/3 cup of apple mixture over one corner of a wrapper, just below the center.
5. Fold the bottom corner over filling.
6. With wet fingers, moisten the remaining wrapper edges.
7. Fold side corners toward center over filling.
8. Roll egg roll up tightly and with your fingers, press at tip to seal.
9. Repeat with the remaining wrappers, cream cheese and filling.
10. Arrange the rolls onto a cooking tray and spray with the cooking spray.
11. Arrange the drip pan in the bottom of Instant Vortex Plus Air Fryer Oven cooking chamber.
12. Select "Air Fry" and then adjust the temperature to 400 degrees F.
13. Set the timer for 12 minutes and press the "Start".
14. When the display shows "Add Food" insert the cooking tray in the center position.

15. When the display shows "Turn Food" turn the rolls and spray with the cooking spray.
16. Meanwhile, in a shallow dish, mix together the sugar and remaining cinnamon.
17. When cooking time is complete, remove the tray from Vortex.
18. Coat the hot egg rolls with sugar mixture and serve.

Nutritional Information per Serving:

- Calories 236
- Total Fat 5.7 g
- Saturated Fat 3.3 g
- Cholesterol 19 mg
- Sodium 229 mg
- Total Carbs 43.3 g
- Fiber 3 g
- Sugar 20.5 g
- Protein 4.5 g

Cinnamon Donuts

Preparation Time: 15 minutes
Cooking Time: 6 minutes
Servings: 8

Ingredients:

- ½ cup granulated sugar
- 1 tablespoon ground cinnamon
- 1 (16.3-ounce) can flaky large biscuits
- Olive oil cooking spray
- 4 tablespoons unsalted butter, melted

Method:

1. Line a baking sheet with parchment paper.
2. In a shallow dish, mix together the sugar and cinnamon. Set aside.
3. Remove the biscuits from the can and carefully, separate them.
4. Place the biscuits onto the prepared baking sheet and with a 1-inch round biscuit cutter, cut holes from the center of each biscuit.
5. Place 4 donuts onto the lightly greased cooking pan in a single layer.
6. Arrange the drip pan in the bottom of Instant Vortex Plus Air Fryer Oven cooking chamber.
7. Select "Air Fry" and then adjust the temperature to 350 degrees F.
8. Set the timer for 6 minutes and press the "Start".
9. When the display shows "Add Food" insert the cooking tray in the center position.
10. When the display shows "Turn Food" turn the donuts.
11. When cooking time is complete, remove the tray from Vortex.
12. Brush both sides of the warm donuts with melted butter and then, coat with cinnamon sugar.
13. Repeat with the remaining donuts.
14. Serve warm.

Nutritional Information per Serving:

- Calories 289
- Total Fat 14.3 g
- Saturated Fat 5.5 g
- Cholesterol 15 mg
- Sodium 590 mg
- Total Carbs 36.9 g
- Fiber 1.4 g
- Sugar 15.4 g
- Protein 3.9 g

Chocolate Pastries

Preparation Time: 20 minutes
Cooking Time: 10 minutes
Servings: 4

Ingredients:

- 8 ounces frozen puff pastry, thawed
- 4 tablespoons hazelnut spread
- 4 teaspoons slivered almonds plus more for topping
- 1 egg, beaten
- 1 tablespoon water
- 2 tablespoons turbinado sugar

Method:

1. Place the puff pastry onto a lightly floured surface and unfold it.
2. Cut pastry into 4 squares.
3. Place 1 tablespoon of hazelnut spread on each square and top with almonds.
4. With wet fingers, moisten the edges of each pastry and fold into a rectangle shape.
5. With a fork, press the edges to seal.
6. In a small bowl, add the egg and 1 tablespoon of water and beat well.
7. Coat the top of each pastry with the egg wash and sprinkle with turbinado sugar, followed by a few slivered almonds.
8. Arrange the pastries onto 2 cooking trays.
9. Arrange the drip pan in the bottom of Instant Vortex Plus Air Fryer Oven cooking chamber.
10. Select "Air Fry" and then adjust the temperature to 330 degrees F.
11. Set the timer for 10 minutes and press the "Start".
12. When the display shows "Add Food" insert 1 tray in the top position and another in the bottom position.
13. When the display shows "Turn Food" do not turn the food but switch the position of cooking trays.
14. When cooking time is complete, remove the trays from Vortex and serve warm.

Nutritional Information per Serving:

- Calories 452
- Total Fat 29.7 g

- Saturated Fat 7.5 g
- Cholesterol 41 mg
- Sodium 168 mg
- Total Carbs 40.5 g

- Fiber 1.6 g
- Sugar 14.5 g
- Protein 7.1 g

Strawberry Danish

Preparation Time: 20 minutes
Cooking Time: 25 minutes
Servings: 6

Ingredients:

- 1 tube full-sheet crescent roll dough
- 4 ounces cream cheese, softened
- ¼ cup strawberry jam
- ½ cup fresh strawberries, hulled and chopped
- 1 cup confectioner's sugar
- 2-3 tablespoons cream

Method:

1. Place the sheet of crescent roll dough onto a flat surface and unroll it.
2. In a microwave-safe bowl, add the cream cheese and microwave for about 20-30 seconds,
3. Remove from microwave and stir until creamy and smooth.
4. Spread the cream cheese over the dough sheet, followed by the strawberry jam.
5. Now, place the strawberry pieces evenly across the top.
6. From the short side, roll the dough and pinch the seam to seal.
7. Arrange a greased parchment paper ono the cooking tray.
8. Carefully, curve the rolled pastry into a horseshoe shape and arrange onto the prepared tray.
9. Arrange the drip pan in the bottom of Instant Vortex Plus Air Fryer Oven cooking chamber.
10. Select "Air Fry" and then adjust the temperature to 350 degrees F.
11. Set the timer for 25 minutes and press the "Start".
12. When the display shows "Add Food" insert the cooking tray in the center position.
13. When the display shows "Turn Food" turn the rolls and spray with the cooking spray.
14. Meanwhile, in a shallow dish, mix together the sugar and remaining cinnamon.
15. When cooking time is complete, remove the tray from Vortex and place onto a rack to cool.
16. Meanwhile, in a bowl, mix together the confectioner's sugar and cream.

17. Drizzle the cream mixture over cooled Danish and serve.

Nutritional Information per Serving:

- Calories 338
- Total Fat 13.6 g
- Saturated Fat 7 g
- Cholesterol 22 mg
- Sodium 341 mg

- Total Carbs 48.8 g
- Fiber 0.2 g
- Sugar 4.8 g
- Protein 4.2 g

Homemade Oreos

Preparation Time: 15 minutes
Cooking Time: 4 minutes
Servings: 9

Ingredients:

- 1 crescent sheet roll
- 9 Oreo cookies

Method:

1. Place the sheet of crescent roll dough onto a flat surface and unroll it.
2. With a knife, cut the dough into 9 even squares.
3. Wrap each cookie in 1 dough square completely.
4. Arrange the Oreos onto a cooking tray.
5. Arrange the drip pan in the bottom of Instant Vortex Plus Air Fryer Oven cooking chamber.
6. Select "Air Fry" and then adjust the temperature to 360 degrees F.
7. Set the timer for 4 minutes and press the "Start".
8. When the display shows "Add Food" insert the cooking tray in the center position.
9. When the display shows "Turn Food" turn the Oreos.
10. When cooking time is complete, remove the tray from Vortex.
11. Serve warm.

Nutritional Information per Serving:

- Calories 137
- Total Fat 6.4 g
- Saturated Fat 2.2 g
- Cholesterol 0 mg
- Sodium 237 mg
- Total Carbs 17.1 g
- Fiber 0.3 g
- Sugar 6.8 g
- Protein 2.3 g

Chocolate Brownies

Preparation Time: 15 minutes
Cooking Time: 15 minutes
Servings: 4

Ingredients:

- ½ cup all-purpose flour
- ¾ cup sugar
- 6 tablespoons unsweetened cocoa powder
- ¼ teaspoon baking powder
- ¼ teaspoon salt
- ¼ cup unsalted butter, melted
- 2 large eggs
- 1 tablespoon vegetable oil
- ½ teaspoon vanilla extract

Method:

1. Grease a 7-inch baking pan generously. Set aside.
2. In a bowl, add all the ingredients and mix until well combined.
3. Place the mixture into the prepared baking pan and with the back of a poon, smooth the top surface.
4. Arrange the drip pan in the bottom of Instant Vortex Plus Air Fryer Oven cooking chamber.
5. Select "Air Fry" and then adjust the temperature to 330 degrees F.
6. Set the timer for 15 minutes and press the "Start".
7. When the display shows "Add Food" place the baking pan over the drip pan.
8. When the display shows "Turn Food" do nothing.
9. When cooking time is complete, remove the pan from Vortex and place onto a wire rack to cool completely before cutting.
10. Cut the brownie into desired-sized squares and serve.

Nutritional Information per Serving:

- Calories 385
- Total Fat 18.7g
- Saturated Fat 9.4 g
- Cholesterol 124 mg
- Sodium 266 mg
- Total Carbs 54.3 g
- Fiber 3.1 g
- Sugar 38 g
- Protein 6.5 g

Rum Cake

Preparation Time: 15 minutes
Cooking Time: 25 minutes
Servings: 6

Ingredients:

- ½ package yellow cake mix
- ½ (3.4-ounce) package Jell-O instant pudding
- 2 eggs
- ¼ cup vegetable oil
- ¼ cup water
- ¼ cup dark rum

Method:

1. In a bowl, add all the ingredients and with an electric mixer, beat until well combined.
2. Arrange a parchment paper in the bottom of a greased 8-inch pan.
3. Now, arrange a foil piece around the cake pan.
4. Place the mixture into the prepared baking pan and with the back of a poon, smooth the top surface.
5. Arrange the drip pan in the bottom of Instant Vortex Plus Air Fryer Oven cooking chamber.
6. Select "Air Fry" and then adjust the temperature to 325 degrees F.
7. Set the timer for 25 minutes and press the "Start".
8. When the display shows "Add Food" place the baking pan over the drip pan.
9. When the display shows "Turn Food" do nothing.
10. When cooking time is complete, remove the pan from Vortex and place onto a wire rack to cool for about 10 minutes.
11. Carefully, invert the cake onto wire rack to cool completely before cutting.
12. Cut into desired-sized slices and serve.

Nutritional Information per Serving:

- Calories 315
- Total Fat 14.9 g
- Saturated Fat 2.9 g
- Cholesterol 55 mg
- Sodium 613 mg
- Total Carbs 36.5 g
- Fiber 0.4 g
- Sugar 16.5 g
- Protein 3.5 g

Blueberry Cobbler

Preparation Time: 15 minutes
Cooking Time: 20 minutes
Servings: 6

Ingredients:

For Filling:

- 2½ cups fresh blueberries
- 1 teaspoon vanilla extract
- 1 teaspoon fresh lemon juice
- 1 cup sugar
- 1 teaspoon flour
- 1 tablespoon butter, melted

For Topping:

- 1¾ cups all-purpose flour
- 6 tablespoons sugar
- 4 teaspoons baking powder
- 1 cup milk
- 5 tablespoons butter

For Sprinkling:

- 2 teaspoons sugar
- ¼ teaspoon ground cinnamon

Method:

1. For filling: in a bowl, add all the ingredients and mix until well combined.
2. In another large bowl, mix together the flour, baking powder, and sugar.
3. Add the milk and butter and mix until a crumply mixture forms.
4. For sprinkling: in a small bowl mix together the sugar and cinnamon.
5. In the bottom of a greased pan, place the blueberries mixture and top with the flour mixture evenly.
6. Sprinkle the cinnamon sugar on top evenly.

7. Arrange the drip pan in the bottom of Instant Vortex Plus Air Fryer Oven cooking chamber.
8. Select "Air Fry" and then adjust the temperature to 320 degrees F.
9. Set the timer for 20 minutes and press the "Start".
10. When the display shows "Add Food" place the baking pan over the drip pan.
11. When the display shows "Turn Food" do nothing.
12. When cooking time is complete, remove the pan from Vortex and place onto a wire rack to cool for about 10 minutes before serving.

Nutritional Information per Serving:

- Calories 459
- Total Fat 12.6 g
- Saturated Fat 7.8 g
- Cholesterol 34 mg
- Sodium 105 mg

- Total Carbs 84 g
- Fiber 2.7 g
- Sugar 53.6 g
- Protein 5.5 g

Chapter 9: Meal Plan for 30 Days

Day 1

Breakfast: Nuts & Seeds Granola

Lunch: Seasoned Potatoes

Dinner: Roasted Spicy Chicken

Day 2

Breakfast: Egg & Cheese Puffs

Lunch: Buttered Cauliflower

Dinner: Seasoned Beef Roast

Day 3

Breakfast: Breakfast Egg Rolls

Lunch: BBQ Chicken Wings

Dinner: Lemony Shrimp

Day 4

Breakfast: Simple Bagels

Lunch: Tuna Burgers

Dinner: Crusted Rack of Lamb

Day 5

Breakfast: Sausage & Bacon Omelet

Lunch: Green Beans with Carrots

Dinner: Garlicky Pork Tenderloin

Day 6

Breakfast: Sausage with Eggs

Lunch: Spiced Zucchini

Dinner: Breaded Chicken Breast

Day 7

Breakfast: Veggies Frittata

Lunch: Lamb Burgers

Dinner: Spiced Pork Shoulder

Day 8

Breakfast: Nuts & Seeds Granola

Lunch: Mixed Veggie Combo

Dinner: Bacon Wrapped Filet Mignon

Day 9

Breakfast: Breakfast Egg Rolls

Lunch: Crispy Shrimp

Dinner: Seasoned Pork Tenderloin

Day 10

Breakfast: French Toast Sticks

Lunch: Vinegar Brussels Sprout

Dinner: Simple Turkey Breast

Day 11

Breakfast: Egg & Cheese Puffs

Lunch: Lamb Burgers

Dinner: Breaded Cod

Day 12

Breakfast: Sausage & Bacon Omelet

Lunch: Simple Asparagus

Dinner: Spicy Chicken Legs

Day 13

Breakfast: Egg, Bacon & Cheese Puffs

Lunch: Thyme Potatoes

Dinner: Seasoned Pork Chops

Day 14

Breakfast: Sausage & Bacon Omelet

Lunch: Spiced Zucchini

Dinner: Bacon Wrapped Filet Mignon

Day 15

Breakfast: Egg, Bacon & Cheese Puffs

Lunch: BBQ Chicken Wings

Dinner: Spicy Tilapia

Day 16

Breakfast: Veggies Frittata

Lunch: Crab Cakes

Dinner: Glazed Pork Tenderloin

Day 17

Breakfast: Simple Bagels

Lunch: Beef Burgers

Dinner: Spiced Chicken Thighs

Day 18

Breakfast: Sausage with Eggs

Lunch: Parmesan Broccoli

Dinner: Herbed Turkey Breast

Day 19

Breakfast: Nuts & Seeds Granola

Lunch: Green Beans with Potatoes

Dinner: Crispy Haddock

Day 20

Breakfast: Egg, Bacon & Cheese Puffs

Lunch: Simple Asparagus

Dinner: Crusted Rack of Lamb

Day 21

Breakfast: French Toast Sticks

Lunch: Buttered Cauliflower

Dinner: Spicy Chicken Legs

Day 22

Breakfast: Egg & Cheese Puffs

Lunch: Crispy Shrimp

Dinner: Breaded Pork Chops

Day 23

Breakfast: French Toast Sticks

Lunch: Lamb Burgers

Dinner: Spiced Chicken Thighs

Day 24

Breakfast: Breakfast Egg Rolls

Lunch: Seasoned Potatoes

Dinner: Seasoned Beef Roast

Day 25

Breakfast: Simple Bagels

Lunch: Beef Burgers

Dinner: Herbed Turkey Breast

Day 26

Breakfast: French Toast Sticks

Lunch: Beef Burgers

Dinner: Lemony Salmon

Day 27

Breakfast: Veggies Frittata

Lunch: Crab Cakes

Dinner: Honey Mustad Pork Tenderloin

Day 28

Breakfast: Sausage & Bacon Omelet

Lunch: Vinegar Brussels Sprout

Dinner: Lemony Salmon

Day 29

Breakfast: Nuts & Seeds Granola

Lunch: Thyme Potatoes

Dinner: Simple Beef Sirloin Roast

Day 30

Breakfast: Sausage with Eggs

Lunch: Parmesan Broccoli

Dinner: Buttermilk Roasted Chicken

Conclusion

With the Instant Vortex Air Fryer Oven, smart cooking has now become a new reality. This appliance came as a relief for all the chefs and homemakers, who can now cook delicious crispy meals in no time. The Instant vortex technology has brought more efficiency into an electric oven. It guarantees even cooking every time. So, if you are planning to bring this kitchen marvel home, then don't wait around and give it a try with the range of flavorsome recipes shared in this cookbook.